THE WOUNDED HEALER

Though countertransference – what really happens in the internal world of the analyst – is considered by many to be the core issue in depth psychology and psychoanalysis today, there have been few extended studies of the process. David Sedgwick's study candidly presents the therapist's countertransference struggles in an ongoing fashion, and shows how the analyst is, as Jung said, "as much in the analysis as the patient."

Jung was one of the first analysts to stress the therapeutic potential of countertransference. *The Wounded Healer* extends Jung's ideas to create a new, dynamic view of countertransference processes. It stresses the importance of the analyst's own woundedness and how this may be used to aid the patient.

Beginning with a discussion of the need and justification for a Jungian approach to countertransference, the book reviews Jungian theories and presents detailed illustrations of cases showing the complexity of the processes in both the patient and analyst. David Sedgwick concludes with a model of countertransference processing. *The Wounded Healer* will be particularly important for all clinicians and students interested in the struggles of the therapeutic process.

David Sedgwick is a Jungian analyst in Charlottesville, Virginia, and is also a clinical psychologist and assistant professor at the University of Virginia. He is the author of *Jung and Searles: A comparative study.*

Also available from Routledge

JUNG AND SEARLES
A comparative study
David Sedgwick

SHAME AND THE ORIGINS OF SELF-ESTEEM
A Jungian approach
Mario Jacoby

JUNG AND EASTERN THOUGHT
A dialogue with the Orient
J.J. Clarke

JUNG AND THE MONOTHEISMS
Judaism, Christianity, Islam
Edited by Joel Ryce-Menuhin

ANALYSIS ANALYSED
Fred Plaut

THE WOUNDED HEALER

Countertransference from a Jungian perspective

David Sedgwick

London and New York

First published 1994
by Routledge
11 New Fetter Lane, London EC4P 4EE
Simultaneously published in the USA and Canada
by Routledge
29 West 35th Street, New York, NY 10001

Typeset in Palatino by LaserScript Limited, Mitcham, Surrey
Printed and bound in Great Britain by
Mackays of Chatham PLC, Chatham, Kent

British Library Cataloguing in Publication Data
A catalogue record for this book is available from the British Library

Library of Congress Cataloging in Publication Data
A catalogue record for this book has been applied for

ISBN 0–415–10619–2 (hbk)
ISBN 0–415–10620–6 (pbk)

TO CAROLYN

CONTENTS

CONTENTS

ACKNOWLEDGMENTS

Many people – almost too many to acknowledge – contributed in various ways to this book on countertransference. However, special thanks are due to Steve Hill, Lois Harvey and Judy Savage, who generously contributed original ideas, detailed feedback and time during the writing process. Andrew Samuels helped me clarify parts of the manuscript and was supportive in general, as was the editorial staff at Routledge.

Writing this book marked the culmination of my analytic training with the Inter-regional Society of Jungian Analysts. Members of that society who supervised or otherwise taught me things (and thus influenced this book) include Alex McCurdy, Lois Harvey, Ron Kledzik, Julia McAfee, Del McNeely, Terrence Lee, Rosales Wynne-Roberts, John Talley, Don Williams and Gene Monick, not to mention my fellow candidates and many other analysts along the way.

This book continues and specifies lines of thought evolved in my first book, which was a comparison of the theories of C.G. Jung and Harold F. Searles. This study of countertransference processes owes much to that earlier book and, of course, to the writings of those two men.

I would like to express my special gratitude to the patients mentioned in this book, who must go unnamed, for allowing me to write about them and learn from them.

I am astonished, disappointed, pleased with myself. I am distressed, depressed, rapturous. I am all these things at once, and cannot add up the sum . . . . There is nothing I am quite sure about . . . . I exist on the foundation of something I do not know.

C.G. Jung

Everything, however, gets smaller on its way to becoming eternal.

Norman Maclean

1

INTRODUCTION

This is the first Jungian book exclusively on countertransference. Its purpose is to show what countertransference – the analyst's subjective involvement in the psychotherapeutic process – is really like, and how it can be worked with from a Jungian perspective.

The phenomenology of countertransference is rarely discussed in print – for various reasons, some of them valid. This lack of thorough discussion may be defensive, as Little (1951) and other psychoanalysts first suggested 40 years ago[1]. Countertransference sometimes tends to be thought of *in the analyst's fantasy* as impermissible, embarrassing or professionally damaging (to the analyst or to the profession as a whole). Thus the analyst's subjective experience with the patient, which may be the core of in-depth analytic work, has been less well attended to than the patient's experience of the analyst (transference). While attempts to "expose" countertransference may indeed collide with narcissistic–exhibitionistic issues, the "phenomenology of countertransference" is nevertheless of considerable clinical value.

This book is written primarily for psychotherapists and others interested in the therapeutic process. It is not intended for patients, though conceivably it could be informative for them too. It could be disturbing as well. As one female colleague noted, this kind of writing is somewhat like a gynecologist revealing fantasies about patients. Are these things better left unsaid (or at least unwritten)? Perhaps so, as far as the patient is concerned. On the other hand, the subject needs airing because it is real and it is denied, and it is an important topic for professionals.

My interest in countertransference stems from my own experience of strong reactions to patients. For a long time before and after my analytic training, I wondered if my often intense

1

involvements in psychotherapy were a problem, caused perhaps by a poorly boundaried personality, oversensitivity, introversion, neurotic dependency, hyperconscientiousness, or whatever. Gradually, and somewhat reluctantly, I have come to appreciate the fact that patients will have an impact on me. Indeed, an absence of impact may mean as much as its presence. This too is part of countertransference, or can be a stage in it.

Part of the difficulty in writing about countertransference, aside from its burdensome nature, is that countertransference usually carries the negative connotations noted above. One tends to feel guilty. Freud's early dictum about "mastering" countertransference has much to do with this, of course. Even today, mainstream psychotherapy and classical psychoanalysis remain cautious. This may not be inappropriate, in this era of well-publicized ethical and boundary violations by therapists. At the very least, countertransference and its usage therapeutically continue to require care and justification. Perhaps each clinician, coming from a place of initial concern about his/her own "neurotic countertransference," must come then to a more sophisticated, natural relation to this complex area of analytic interchange.

Reticence about countertransference has been lessening in Jungian analytic circles, as it has for a longer time in psychoanalysis. Jung said something very significant when he suggested that the analyst is " . . . as much 'in the analysis' as the patient" (1929a, p. 72). However, the precise meaning of this, as well as its possible clinical implications, were not enlarged upon in detail except by Michael Fordham and the London-based Society of Analytical Psychology group (beginning in the mid-1950s). Neither Jung nor his first wave of followers elucidated his position in a practical, clear way, though they did continue to promote the "dialectical" notion generally. As Harriet Machtiger noted about ten years ago, "Until fairly recently, [Jungian] analysts were largely, or completely, unaware of the importance of the countertransference for the outcome of therapy" (1982, p. 107).

With this gradual change in "awareness" in the last decade has come an increased volume of Jungian written material, which supplements the pioneering work in London. It would now probably be the rule rather than the exception for Jungian analysts and analytic candidates to attend, at least, to transference phenomena. And with a transference orientation of any type, issues of the analyst's countertransference soon arise (or should), as Jung's dialectical notions suggest.

A Jungian analyst's or candidate's task now involves not just an integrated understanding of Jung but also an understanding of the "post-Jungians." In addition, a more thorough integration of non-Jungian psychoanalysts may be in order. For decades British Jungian analysts (Fordham, Hubback, Plaut, Gordon, Redfearn, Lambert, Samuels, et al.) have emphasized Freudian technique and the work of psychoanalytic theorists like Klein, Winnicott, Bion, and Racker. More recently, Jungian analysts have synthesized the work of Kohut (Jacoby, 1981, 1984, 1990; Schwartz-Salant, 1982), Langs (Goodheart, 1980; Parks, 1987) and Searles (Sedgwick, 1993) among others.

A significant aspect of these integrative writings is that they focus primarily on transference dynamics. In general they are part of an effort to fill in the gaps left by Jung's more symbolic, less clinical stance. This "new" focus on transference has also shown evolution over time. At first, as Fordham *et al.* (1974, p. ix) point out, there was an interest, particularly in London, on analysis of *transference* per se. In other words the patient's unconscious projections or reenactments in the analytic hour were paramount. This progressed to a situation where the analyst's reactions, the *countertransference*, were more closely studied for their informational and not just neurotic value. The result has been a blended focus on both sides of the *analyst–patient interaction*. Transference and countertransference are now typically seen in conjunction in Jungian circles, appropriately so. More recent Jungian articles or collections of articles tend to have names or terms like "Transference/Countertransference," "Countertransference/Transference," "T/CT" (e.g. Stein, 1982; Hall, 1984).

This blend, while appropriate, does not necessarily mean that such articles lay the stress on countertransference that this study will. It is often the case that the transference side of the coin – the patient's contribution – receives more attention than the analyst's countertransference contribution (the literature review in the next chapter will tend to confirm this).

Thus Machtiger's 1982 article (see p. 2) accurately emphasizes that it is only "recently" that any awareness of countertransference has been present in most Jungian circles. To explain this reticence, Stein cites the analyst's defensive fears of revealing his or her "unwashed psyche," and seconds Machtiger's call for

3

"a more courageous discussion of countertransference" (Stein, 1984, pp. 67–68). In a more recent article Steinberg, when characterizing countertransference as a sub-topic of "wounded healer" issues, suggests that little has been written on the *specific* wounds of the healer and *how* these might affect analysis (Steinberg, 1989, p. 11). He goes on to say that processes in the analyst need more detailed description.

This book is an attempt to further the discussion and description. It is one thing to take note of countertransference, as analysts increasingly do, and another to really work with it. It is still another matter, perhaps of more than just degree, to assert as Machtiger does that "It is the analyst's reaction in the counter-transference that is the *essential therapeutic factor in analysis*" (Machtiger, 1982, p. 90, italics mine).

The thesis of this book is that countertransference can be used, not only as a secondary technique, but as a *primary* instrument in Jungian analysis. It is on a par with more "traditional" Jungian methods and can be readily coordinated with them. This book will demonstrate in detail a countertransference-based way of working and show the primacy of countertransference as an analytic phenomenon.

This study meets more than the author's personal needs and the calls from contemporary Jungian analysts for deeper studies of countertransference. There are a fair number of what Andrew Samuels in his rigorous examination *Jung and the Post-Jungians* calls "unknowing Jungians" (Samuels, 1985, p. 10). He is referring to the fact that current trends in psychoanalysis and therapy sometimes tend in directions that Jung mapped out in general ways many years before. In particular Samuels mentions the use of countertransference as a therapeutic tool. For those who believe that the Jungian approach has much to offer, it is therefore important that his work does not continue to float outside the psychotherapeutic mainstream. Along these lines it is useful to note that excellent books on countertransference have been published in recent years by psychoanalysts (e.g. Searles, 1979; Epstein and Feiner, 1979; Masterson, 1983; Gorkin, 1987; Tansey and Burke, 1989). Meanwhile, analytical psychology has not produced any book-length studies on the subject[2]. It seems important for the Jungian viewpoint to be addressed in further detail and at book length.

Jung himself is partly to blame for any lagging behind in the delineation of countertransference. As in other technical areas, Jung left the details to his followers. This is understandable, if frustrating. Jung's fertile unconscious did lead him away from the more purely clinical interests of his early professional years (cf. Fordham, 1978a; Goodheart, 1980; Charlton, 1986). Likewise his personal style and typology, as well as his symbolic/archetypal focus, were involved, the latter tending to pull him away from the personal micro-analysis required for countertransference exploration. Besides, there was only so much Jung could do. When asked in his later years why he did not attempt a more systematic presentation of his theories, Jung replied, "Sorry . . . to complete this psychology would take more than a lifetime" (Harms, 1962, p. 732). Thus it is left to Jung's followers to illustrate and further his theories in many areas.

In the realm of countertransference this is both easy and difficult. The difficulty lies in the more impersonal, collective focus Jung took in later writings and his content-over-process emphasis. This is well exemplified in "The Psychology of the Transference" (Jung, 1946), his definitive work on the subject. This treatise is an extremely important but almost exclusively *symbolic* amplification of transference phenomena via alchemical imagery. On the positive side, it has provided a vital jumping-off point for later Jungian ventures into the subject (e.g. Groesbeck, 1975; Schwartz-Salant, 1984). The alchemical symbols are vivid and evocative – one senses their power and parallels with actual analytic material.

However, Jung's opus is virtually devoid of clinical examples. It begs for the grounding in therapeutic reality that a practical example would give. The unconscious material in impersonal form (in this case the fantasies of alchemists) is given prominence over the "personal," just as it is in Jung's extended case studies[3].

On the other hand, as noted above, Jung leaves it to the involved reader to fill in the blanks. While somewhat tantalizing, his ideas and suggestions can be excellent guideposts. One can return repeatedly to "The Psychology of the Transference" to find value in Jung's alchemical symbols and perspective. He may not mention the word "countertransference"[4] but he notes the centrality of the analyst's psyche. He comments on psychic infection, wounded healing and the analyst "literally taking over" the patient's sufferings. He speaks of mutual analyst–patient influence and transformation. Psychic contents flash back and forth mercurially between the participants.

Mercurial and ever-changing himself, Jung fluctuated over time in his evaluation of transference itself (and therefore countertransference). This too may have contributed to a certain delay by his followers in following up on his astute hypotheses about the analytic interaction. Naturally his original, 1907 "alpha and omega" point of view on transference was closely tied to his early relationship with Freud (Jung, 1946, p. 172). After the break with Freud, Jung (1929a, 1935b) gradually evolved his innovative ideas about the importance of the analyst's side of the equation (i.e. the countertransference). Yet in the 1935 Tavistock Lectures he strikes a distinctly skeptical, almost reactionary note: "Transference or no transference, that has nothing to do with the cure . . . . The dreams bring out everything that is necessary" (Jung, 1935a, p. 136)[5]. His ambivalence continues in his official 1946 work[6] on the subject. However, his final written statement is that transference (again meaning, for Jung, the *mixtum compositum* of analyst and patient) is the "crux, or at any rate the crucial experience, in any thoroughgoing analysis" (Jung, 1958, p. vii).

All this points to the need for a book that emphasizes the primacy of countertransference. Again, however, it is this author's personal interest in the topic that is generating the book. Jung himself said we must recognize that all psychologies, including his own, involve a "subjective confession" (Jung, 1929b, p. 336). This study will embody that idea – almost literally, as it turns out. Following a review and discussion of Jungian perspectives on countertransference (starting with Jung himself), the book will show the workings of the author's inner processes as they move in conjunction (or sometimes disjunction) with the movements in patients. Jung's own extended case examples (see Note 3) show gradual developments in his patients over time and in that sense provide a structure for this study. Here, in addition to the patient's fantasies, conflicts and dreams, the author will also show some of his own. In this way what Jung (1946, p. 171) termed the chemical "combination" of patient and analyst can be more fully elucidated.

Such "subjective confessions" do not come easily. At times it may seem that the old joke applies: "Psychotherapy is when two people who need help get it." As earlier Jungian writers, hesitating before writing about their countertransferences, have said, "One seldom likes to expose oneself in public" (Frantz, 1971, p. 148) or "[one feels] indecent if he talks too much about himself" (Blomeyer, 1974, p. 97). Yet it is just such disclosures that recent authors demand (see pp. 3–4) and that Jung seemed to encourage when he insisted:

> We have learned to place in the foreground the personality of the doctor himself as the curative or harmful factor; . . . what is now demanded is his own transformation – the self-education of the educator.
>
> (Jung, 1929a, p. 74)

Following the discussion of Jungian approaches to date and the case material will be some conclusions. The themes mentioned in the case examples will be drawn together. Some of the viewpoints presented by previous writers on the subject will be modified and this author's overall understandings of countertransference noted. The goal, again, is to establish that there is a way of doing Jungian analysis that is based on monitoring and working with the analyst's countertransference. To this end I will show in more detail than usual the actual processing that takes place, the nuts and bolts of a countertransference-based way of working. This should shed light on the real implications of Jung's assertions that the patient and analyst are *both* in the analysis and that the analyst's getting right with himself – the "rainmaker" idea (Jung, 1955–56) – can have a crucial transformative effect on the patient.

2

JUNGIAN APPROACHES TO COUNTERTRANSFERENCE: A REVIEW

Jungian literature on countertransference is rather sparse, at least in comparison to psychoanalytic writings. As noted earlier, Jung used the word itself only a few times in his entire collected works. Nor do his early, "first generation" followers have much to say about it. In-depth case studies from early Jungians are hard to find and those that exist aside from Jung's are, like Jung's, without countertransference reference[1].

However Jung's non-use of the word did not mean he ignored the subject. While sometimes appearing to be anti-clinical or anti-technique, Jung was primarily *anti-jargon*. Here he was probably reacting to Freudian viewpoints and language, but Jung almost always theorized in non-medical metaphor. He preferred to let the unconscious speak in its own, naturally "colorful . . . primitive" style (Jung, 1961b, p. 205). Thus alchemy became his metaphor of choice for describing countertransference/transference issues. Alchemical motifs were indirectly supplemented by rich images or myths of wounded healers, shamans, "rainmakers," and religious healing (confession).

Jung's views on countertransference, then, must sometimes be teased out in order to be understood. When this is done, the work of his followers on "countertransference" per se – work which really began in the late 1950s at the end of Jung's life – can be seen as part and parcel of his original concepts. Modern Jungian authors may make more, or less, use of the metaphors that Jung preferred, but their approaches still have a recognizably "Jungian" feel. Jung's breadth of interest and style, as well as his sometimes variable statements, provide his followers with plenty of latitude.

Just as Jung's views must to some extent be derived from his

8

contradictory statements or symbolic focus, so at times must later Jungians' views. Countertransference is not always mentioned by name, or is defined in different ways. Therefore this review contains some derivative theories. Furthermore, this review is limited by nature to published views on countertransference. It is likely, particularly recently, that a much wider discussion of the issue takes place – in supervised "control" work, personal analysis, conference or consultation – than is evident from the quantity of literature. Only in recent years have there been increased and sufficient outlets for written Jungian studies.

This chapter will place some individual studies within larger groups that might be called "schools." However it is important to remember that such schools may not really exist. For example, while it may be fair to say a "London" school on countertransference exists (in a broad sense), it may not be true that, let's say, a "Berlin" school actually exists. Likewise, categorizations within a "Langsian" or a "Wounded Healer" perspective are strictly a creation by this author or others. There has not been enough written in many cases to create actual "schools of thought;" one can aggrandize things or create false schools by virtue of grouping them. For the most part authors are following their own independent trains of thought and experience. It can be slightly, if unintentionally, misleading to link and/or include authors who have written only one article with a certain "school" (see Samuels, 1985). Still, there are threads.

Because of the natural diversity of the Jungian approach and the varying outputs, this section will list relevant studies in chronological order. There appears to be a natural grouping by *decade* though there are sub-trends within each. Starting in the late 1950s, but especially in the 1960s, the work of the London/SAP group is paramount. Their work continues to be refined, of course, but the 1970s are highlighted by new additions from Berlin (Dieckmann, Blomeyer) and by what Samuels (1985) nicely characterizes as a "wounded-healer" group (Guggenbuhl-Craig, Groesbeck). The 1980s are heralded by Machtiger's (1982) previously mentioned call for primary attention to countertransference, the emergence of the first Jungian quasi-academic textbooks written for a wider professional public (Stein, 1982; Samuels, 1985), and a new clinical journal, *Chiron*[2]. The key figures of the 1980s are Goodheart, Jacoby and Schwartz-Salant, each with a different perspective on countertransference. Movements into the 1990s seem to be presaged by the works of Samuels in the mid- and late 1980s and Steinberg (1989) more recently.

JUNG ON COUNTERTRANSFERENCE

Jung appears to be the first analyst of any type to employ countertransference as a therapeutic technique. This is little known, and significant for the history of psychotherapy and Jung's place in it.[3]

Jung spoke of countertransference in many different ways. Early in his work he described it in a straightforward clinical manner. Later he emphasized the engagement of analyst and patient in an archetypal, mutually transformative process. As noted above, Jung elucidated this complex analytic interaction via ideas and examples from chemistry, anthropology, alchemy, medicine (infection, contagion), mythological and shamanistic healing (the "wounded physician"), and eastern religion (Taoism – the "rainmaker"). In addition to these areas where the emotional involvement of the analyst is directly stated or implied, Jung's conceptions around intuition, empathy, dream interpretation on the objective level, analytic style and synchronicity all have bearing on countertransference.

In keeping with his early countertransference focus, Jung (1913, 1929a, 1935b) was the first psychoanalyst to insist that analysts should themselves be analyzed before practicing, a necessity that was acknowledged by Freud (see Freud, 1912; Ellenberger, 1970). This emphasis on what would later be called "training analysis" had a number of corollary implications.

First was the idea that the analysand could progress only as far as the analyst himself had been analyzed (Jung, 1913, p. 198). In a negative sense this meant that the analyst's own "blind" spots could limit or even defensively divert the treatment. Therefore the therapist was "just as responsible for the cleanness of his hands as the surgeon" (Jung, 1914, p. 260). Implied here is not just a limitation but a danger – the analyst could *contaminate* the patient during this psychological surgery. He could make the patient sick.

But Jung says more. A dynamic and potentially positive aspect of the "clean hands" viewpoint is that the patient *identifies* with the analyst in a very personal way. Jung reveals the "open secret" that patients somehow look "into the soul" of the analyst, thereby finding out how the analyst himself handles his own problems and if he practices what he preaches (Jung, 1913, p. 198)[4]. This amounts to a kind of integrity check on the analyst, which is probably done unconsciously and intuitively. As Jung puts it, "The patient *reads* the personality of the analyst, . . . for nothing is finer than the empathy of a neurotic" (Jung, 1914, p. 277).

Jung is at this point suggesting a very subtle unconscious interaction between analyst and patient, one that will later be extended and refined in his writings. The patient, with his finely tuned "empathy," will sense things in and about the analyst. Thus Jung is implying that the involvement of the analyst is inevitable, though potentially dangerous. Furthermore, Jung states that this delicate engagement is crucially involved in the "resolution of the transference" stage of the analysis (Jung, 1913, p. 199). Accordingly, he also says for the first time (and will later state exclusively) that the analyst's "personality is one of the main factors in the cure" (Jung, 1914, p. 260).

These first suggestions become the cornerstones of Jung's attitude toward countertransference. From the idea of training analysis and having "clean hands" comes the later concept that during treatment "the doctor is as much 'in the analysis' as the patient" (Jung, 1929a, p. 72). The notion of the analyst's initial training analysis thus takes on a continuous, in-session quality. From the idea that the patient may intuit the analyst's own ways of approaching problems comes the concept that the analyst should not, and indeed cannot, remain unaffected by the patient. Citing the "reciprocal influence" of patient and therapist, Jung notes that a persona-based "smokescreen of fatherly and pro-fessional authority" only deprives the analyst of "the use of a highly important organ of information" (p. 71) – that is, his counter-transference.

Some of Jung's few uses of the word "countertransference" are in this context, incidentally. He gives here virtually his only definition of the term, calling it a "symptom" of the patient's transference. Jung means something different than a reactive, *counter*-transference to the patient's transference, however. He means the actual transferring, via the aforementioned uncon-scious "influence," of the patient's illness ("symptom") to the analyst (Jung, 1929a, p. 72). This fairly radical statement closely resembles current conceptions of projective identification. Along these lines Jung later condemns Freudian couch technique and general theory as vain and anti-therapeutic attempts to "ward

11

off" the patient's infectious influence (Jung, 1946, p. 171). Whether this criticism is valid or not, it is plain that the effects (or affects) of the patient are highly potent. The analyst's reactions to, or introjections of, such affects are what is normally called countertransference.

Blended with and following from the above comes the idea that the analyst's personality is *the* "main factor in the cure," not just one of many. As Jung states, "We have learned to place in the foreground the personality of the doctor himself as a curative or harmful factor" (Jung, 1929a, p. 74). The analyst's psychology is in the forefront not only in the "clean hands" sense (so as not to infect) but in the receptive sense (to be influenced and even infected himself, in fact). Jung puts it best by saying that the analyst "quite literally 'takes over' the sufferings of his patient and shares them with him" (Jung, 1946, p. 172). It is at this point that "mutual transformation" of both analytic participants becomes the issue, and it is here that Jung brings into play his more vivid metaphorical expressions to describe the process.

In his descriptions of analysis as a "dialectical" or "reciprocal" process between equal parties, Jung on at least two occasions compares this to the combining of two chemical substances in a kind of analytic test tube (Jung, 1929a, 1946). The mixture or "combination" of these elements results in (and paradoxically is also the result of) the alteration of each element and the creation of a new, third compound. This chemical model, while generally appropriate, does not account for the deeper complexity of the chemical interaction. I think Jung would be the first to say that each element has within it many, if not infinite, smaller elements – complexes, for example. Thus he needed a more sophisticated and lyrical analogy to describe the unconscious intermingling of analyst and patient. He found this in alchemy.

The symbolism of alchemy, particularly of the "coniunctio" or "mystic marriage" of the elements in the effort to make gold, seemed to Jung to bear an uncanny resemblance to individuation and transference/countertransference processes. The archetypal mechanisms underlying all three were best embodied in a 1550 alchemical text called the *Rosarium Philosophorum*, upon which Jung based his definitive work on transference, "The Psychology of the Transference" (1946).

While this work does not delineate countertransference in detail, it does present Jung's general ideas and gives some of the feel and experience of the Jungian analyst's side of the (alchemical) equation. First the overall situation is imaged as the analyst and patient, like the alchemical "adept" and "soror," both deeply involved in a psychological laboratory trying to create the "gold." As they experiment with and observe the elements, so to speak, it becomes evident that they themselves are intermingling. Each has his or her respective conscious and unconscious parts, which in turn pull on each other. The central connection is between the unconscious aspects of each and their mutual attraction. This is the heart of the countertransference/transference.

The intermingling of the unconsciouses of each participant – the anima of the male and animus of the female – is then imaged by the Rosarium series. This series shows the "King" and "Queen" gradually getting in touch with each other (first clothed and then naked), uniting sexually (the *coniunctio*), then dying – out of which comes a small person (the soul), which ascends and returns, resulting in the final rebirth/creation of the "hermaphrodite" or Self. This final androgynous development corresponds to the reborn wholeness of the patient.

The superficial description here does not fully portray the subtlety of the imagery or of the archetypal operations underlying the analyst/patient relationship as envisioned by Jung. Jung amplifies his text and the series with further amplifications from fairy tales, anthropology (the cross-cousin marriage) and other alchemical texts. He is at his best clinically, in my opinion, when describing with words some of the characteristics of the process as experienced by the therapist.

He notes specifically that it is the destiny or fate of the analyst to be psychologically infected by the patient, and this should be accepted as such (Jung, 1946, p. 177). In other words, a strong countertransference is the average, expectable condition of Jungian analysis. The analyst, then, must bring to analysis not just his receptivity, but his trained consciousness and relatively intact (one hopes) mental health. For at times the analyst will also be perplexed, psychically threatened, caught in the same "fog" that the patient is caught in (and has "induced" in the analyst). As Jung puts it:

> often the doctor is in much the same position as the alchemist who no longer knew whether he was melting the mysterious amalgam in the crucible or whether he was the

13

salamander glowing in the fire. Psychological induction inevitably causes the two parties to get involved in the transformation of the third and to be themselves transformed in the process, and all the time the doctor's knowledge, like a flickering lamp, is the one dim light in the darkness.

(Jung, 1946, p. 199)

Again, this inchoate condition is the fate of the analyst who by "voluntarily and consciously taking over the psychic sufferings of the patient, exposes himself to the overpowering contents of the unconscious" (Jung, 1946, p. 176). Both participants are in a sense overwhelmed and submerged in the potent, alchemical bath.

Despite all this rich, suggestive imagery, one of the more difficult things is to specify the nature of "the elusive, deceptive, ever-changing content" that shuttles around and through the analytic encounter. Jung likes the alchemical characterization of it as Mercurius, "the wily god of revelation" (Jung, 1946, p. 188), but does not disclose its true nature except to note that it is both demon and deity. It is evident from this mystery that what analyst and patient are working on is in fact that mystery of mysteries, the Self. Hence the difficulty in its direct description.

In other, later works Jung helps bring this down to earth a bit more. "The Psychology of the Transference" turns out to be Jung's greatest amplification of the topic, if not his best explication of it. The countertransference theme of the analyst's own participation in a quasi-mutual treatment receives still more emphasis in Jung's 1951 work, "The Fundamental Questions of Psychotherapy." There is a slight but crucial shift in this study: Jung places even greater importance on the analyst's involvement, but less emphasis on his "mental health" (in the usual sense). At this point it is the analyst's own *suffering* that Jung focuses on. Jung still stresses the "clean hands" and dialectical approaches, but has modified them. For example, while promoting training analysis, he notes that "it is far from being an ideal or an absolutely certain means" of purifying the process on the analyst's side (Jung, 1951a, p. 116). Still, Jung soberly adds, "at least it demonstrates the need for self-criticism" and reinforces the analyst's "aptitudes" for self-exploration. Thus for Jung training analysis is something like a very good start for the analyst and, even if it is more than just a start, it is incomplete by nature. The bulk of the work is ongoing and Jung confirms this by stating, "a good half of every treatment that probes at all deeply consists in the doctor's examining himself." This is a significant statement, suggesting the *primary* importance of countertransference reflection – it is at least *half* the analytic agenda.

By heavily accenting the analyst's vulnerability – his wholeness rather than his "clean hands" perfection – Jung deepens the countertransference issue. It is no longer the analyst's openness, "mental health" or "knowledge" that is the major determinant; rather "it is his own *hurt* that gives him the measure of his power to heal" (Jung, 1951a, p. 116, my emphasis). Jung then for the first time (in print) invokes the myth of Asklepios, the "wounded physician." There is the idea here of a healer with an incurable wound, and paradoxically it is that very woundedness that mediates the healing power, as Jung's quote shows.

Still another modification of the first viewpoints on countertransference is shown when Jung indicates that the need for the "dialectical" procedure is fairly common (Jung, 1951a, p. 117). The dialectical approach is no longer demanded only in the "final, extraordinarily tricky stage which is concerned with the resolution of the transference" (Jung, 1913, p. 199).

Jung returns to the "wounded healer" archetype in his last major work, *Mysterium Coniunctionis* (1955–56), and in his autobiography, where he says with some finality, "Only the wounded physician heals" (Jung, 1961a, p. 134). In the later work, Jung for the first time offers examples and simple, practical advice on countertransference. "The therapist must at all times keep watch over himself," Jung says, "over the way he is reacting to his patient" (p. 133). His earlier statements of protest about analysts' resistances to being affected by patients are now straightforward recommendations: "What does the patient mean to me? . . . The doctor is effective only when he himself is affected" (p. 134). It is important that the patient and analyst "become a problem to each other" (p. 143). This could almost be read as a prescription *for* countertransference.

His statements are supplemented by personal examples, for the first time. Jung's interests in parapsychology and synchronicity receive practical application when he describes awakening with a shock when an ex-patient suicided. Similarly, Jung relates an intuitive, prospective dream about a patient whom he had not yet met. Here the use of objective countertransference is used in ways that challenge the norm. Jung reveals still more of his dreams about patients, the cited instances showing Jung either kneeling before or looking up to them in complementary or compensatory fashions (Jung, 1961a, pp. 133, 139). Jung also mentions that he disclosed the dreams and their interpretations to the patients, with positive results. Thus Jung, in his posthumous autobiography, begins to flesh out the pacesetting ideas on countertransference he had been formulating for half a century.

THE LONDON SCHOOL

Around the time that Jung was writing his final, 1951 paper on psychotherapy and his 1961 autobiography, a group of Jungian analysts in London, chiefly under the tutelage of Michael Fordham, was also beginning to differentiate Jungian concepts of countertransference. Their work, at one time considered controversial vis-à-vis "classical" Jungian theory, continues to this day. These analysts were the first not only to come to grips with the lack of a Jungian developmental theory but, as Fordham put it, to "work out the details" of Jung's general "outline" of countertransference (Fordham, 1960, p. 242).

Fordham's writing on countertransference spans four decades, starting with an article in which he expresses astonishment at how little has been written on clinical aspects of transference (Fordham, 1957, p. 111). To fill this gap, he begins by framing a way of working in which the analyst frees himself of a persona-based stance in favor of a position where the analyst responds to the patient with "suitable or adapted therapeutic reactions" (p. 112). While questioning the reality of any distinct demarcation between the personal and collective unconscious, he nevertheless feels that the therapeutic interaction is based on the "therapeutic content" (and archetypal similarity to the patient) of the analyst's psyche.

Fordham's language, developmental and object relations emphasis, and other writings all suggest that the basis of the "adapted response" is more specifically a quasi-maternal one. The general flavor of the described interactions and the "good breast–bad breast," Kleinian motifs that inform them are linked with countertransference positions in which the analyst is "mother," usually the personal mother. The countertransference

16

task of which Fordham speaks has parallels with being a "good enough" mother-analyst in the Winnicottian sense. Accordingly, the analyst's responses, primarily interpretative in Fordham's view, have to be "created *on every occasion* out of his unconscious" (Fordham, 1957, p. 136). This is like the good mother responding quite individually from an empathic sensing of the child's (patient's) needs.

Fordham defines countertransference broadly as "almost any unconscious behavior of the analyst;" he at first hesitates about its centrality but then does suggest that "all analysis is counter-transference-based" (Fordham, 1957, p. 137) in this broad sense and the aforementioned good mothering sense. As in the Kleinian model on which it is based, projective/introjective processes play a key role in the analyst's feeling states and understandings thereof. These unconscious communications give rise to a differentiation of two kinds of countertransference responses by Fordham.

The first type is what he calls "countertransference illusion" and it bears resemblance to classic psychoanalytic (and Jungian – "clean hands") definitions of countertransference. Analysis per se halts in this scenario, as the reactivation in the analyst of past, unresolved unconscious situations *replaces* the therapeutic situation with the patient (Fordham, 1957, p. 138). Fordham sympathetic-ally suggests that this kind of neurotic countertransference is not invariably a disaster, provided the analyst can at least realize, if not integrate, the projection.

The second kind of countertransference is one Fordham calls "syntonic," meaning that the analyst (by virtue of being in a state of "primitive identity" with the patient) introjects and *experiences* aspects of the patient's unconscious. That is, the sometimes alien feelings or roles introspectively sensed by the analyst can be understood as the patient's psyche impacting the analyst directly. Out of a differentiated understanding of such introjects can even-tually come conscious interpretations to the patient (Fordham, 1957, p. 144).

Fordham's delineations much resemble those of the South American psychoanalyst, Heinrich Racker, who in the 1950s intro-duced the concepts of "neurotic," "concordant" and "comple-mentary" countertransferences. The latter two correspond in slightly more specific fashion to Fordham's "syntonic," and the former to Fordham's "illusory" countertransference. Interestingly, their work was developed independently of each other. Jungian analyst Kenneth Lambert (1972) later outlines Racker's ideas still more specifically.

In later works, Fordham continues to amplify his concepts, stressing the indissoluble blend of countertransference with transference and the importance of projective identification. In some ways his ideas build on Jung's and in others are at variance. Nevertheless, Fordham maintains that the syntonic countertransference has the Self as its basis, allowing the analyst to relinquish ego-control. It is the "whole personality" of the analyst, therefore, that permits him to respond or "deintegrate" appropriately to meet the patient's needs of the given analytic moment (Fordham, 1960, p. 249).

He also offers some precise technical recommendations on complex interactions, particularly in response to delusional transferences. For example, there may be times when the patient is in effect analyzing the analyst and the latter may feel that the patient has a point. While the patient may be "correct" in fact, it is also necessary that the analyst explore the patient's motives and/or defenses (Fordham, 1957, 1978b.) In another specific way, Fordham suggests that the analyst's self-disclosures, premature countertransference-based interpretations, amplifications, or pre-scriptions of active imagination or dreamwork can all dilute or defend against the transference (Fordham, 1957, 1969, 1978b). He is outlining here a position of analytic reserve or neutrality within which projective and introjective processes may occur.

Reviewing Jung's analytic style, Fordham raises some questions about Jung's occasional "spontaneity and violence" (nonphysical) in session (Fordham, 1978b, p. 123). Also, in contrast to Jung, Fordham notes that the relationship is in fact "asymmetrical," despite its mutuality: due to his previous analysis, experience and training, the analyst is actually *not* quite "as much in the analysis as the patient" (Fordham, 1978a, p. 86).

In a final step, Fordham crystallizes his thought on countertransference by suggesting that the term be reserved only for those situations where the analyst is blocked or unable to contain patient material. This is close to its original meaning. The rest of the mutual interaction, illusory and otherwise, between participants is best labeled the "analytic dialectic" (Fordham, 1979, p. 644). Thus countertransference/transference is so fundamental as to need redefinition[5].

Fordham's influence extends throughout the London school. However, there are authors whose work precedes his and who complement Fordham's ideas with unique contributions of their own. Robert Moody's (1955) case study of countertransference in child analysis is a pioneering work. After stating that Jung thought countertransference to be as valid therapeutically as transference, Moody asks how the analyst might use the inevitable subjective reactions constellated in treatment. A choice sometimes arises between a "neutral" attitude and one where the analyst leaves his "ego-stronghold" and lets himself be "drawn into a relationship as an active participant" (p. 56). Moody demonstrates the latter with a candid example from a brief child analysis, one in which there is a more spontaneous living out of the "common unconscious" (p. 52) of analyst and patient.

Fred Plaut's (1956) work on "incarnating the archetype" carries forward this theme in an adult context. He suggests that the nature of Jungian analysis, with the analyst in sight and exposed to the patient's "projectiles" (as he amusingly puts it), means the analyst need not deny or disguise his emotional engagement with the patient. As target of the patient's projections, however, a problem arises with regard to irreducible archetypal contents. When they are transferred, the analyst is faced with two alternatives: 1) to elucidate, amplify and/or give back the projection(s) or 2) to "incarnate" (i.e. contain or absorb them) without interpreting them back too soon to the client (Plaut, 1956, p. 156).

As when Fordham infers a Self-reliance in the analytic process, Plaut emphasizes that this "incarnation" process is *not* consciously controlled and therefore the analyst may typically experience some "reluctance" about it. Nor is it easy – a key issue is the "comparative safety" of the analyst (Plaut, 1956, p. 157). He must take care neither to overidentify nor defensively withdraw from the patient's projection. The dangers of inflation or boundary loss are important, for it is frequently *only* in retrospect that the analyst may be able to see clearly what has been happening.

Plaut's idea is based on Jung's notion that the archetypal transference will shift gradually. There are echoes of Jung's *deo concedente* ("god willing") transference approach as well as a nice resonance with Jung on the dangers of an inflation induced by a "savior" projection:

19

Of course the analyst will say, "What nonsense! This is just morbid. It is a hysterical exaggeration." Yet – it tickles him; it is just too nice . . . . So he begins to feel, "If there are saviors, well, perhaps it is just possible that I am one."

(Jung, 1935a, p. 153)

Plaut's ideas also seem to be forerunners of Kohut's (1971, 1977) notions permitting the patient to experience a merger with the *selfobject* analyst in an idealizing transference. It appears as well that the analyst's holding the countertransference position by incarnating rather than interpreting it away fits with Fordham's Winnicottian idea of the patient "calling out" the "adapted therapeutic reactions" he needs from the mother-analyst (Fordham, 1957, p. 112). As Plaut says, "I can then become what the patient's unconscious insists I should be" (Plaut, 1956, p. 157).

The idea of a creative, reparative fantasy process which the analyst engages in receptively is reminiscent of Jung's technique of active imagination. It is as if active imagination is grounded through countertransference participation. While this runs counter to Von Franz' warnings about the dangers of applying active imagination to real people (Von Franz, 1974, p. 76), the risk is here undertaken. Other articles by London Jungians further the concept of an active imaginal/experiential process in the analytic hour itself.

Strauss first of all asserts that the archetypal image has value *only* if bound in personal interaction with the analyst (Strauss, 1960, p. 251). Davidson specifically envisions "transference as a form of active imagination," an idea she derived from countertransference experiences (Davidson, 1966, p. 188). Gordon also characterizes analysis as a "lived through active imagination" between both participants (Gordon, 1968, p. 182). She points out the necessity of discriminating the analyst's *own* reactions from those stimulated by the therapeutic needs of the client. Gordon makes a fine articulation too of a subtle but important type of countertransference movement:

When I begin to notice that I respond in the sessions with, as it were, a wider spectrum of myself, then I take this as a sign that the patient's world has become less stressful . . . more of him there with which to respond to more of me.

(Gordon, 1968, p. 187)

Finally, Cameron (1968) adds a Kleinian-oriented article on "creative illusion" in the transference (including an example of a strong, spontaneous countertransference disclosure à la Jung). In terms of this review, each of these articles, and Fordham's and Plaut's too, have good examples of the analyst's countertransference activity. Not too much is described of the analyst's deeper struggles with the countertransference until Fordham's later work (1978a, 1979) starts to approach it.

Meanwhile, Lambert's (1972) paper on Racker begins to point to some of the possibilities. For Lambert, Racker's work in the 1950s, published in book form in 1968, represents the "first systematic study" in detail of the personal dimension of the analyst–patient dyad (Lambert, 1972, p. 305). *Two* people, not just one (the patient), are involved, each with a healthy and unhealthy part, an adult and childish part, a past and present, etc. Lambert elaborates Racker's "neurotic" countertransference, in which the analyst is identified with his own "infantile" aspects vis-a-vis the patient (or the patient's relatives), society, or professional colleagues. This corresponds to Fordham's "illusory" type. "Countertransference proper" consists of Racker's comfortable "concordant" variety in which analyst and patient share parallel experiences, and the more volatile "complementary" form in which the analyst is induced into identity with one of the patient's "internal objects" (Lambert, 1972, p. 313).

Following up on the "complementary" type, Lambert adds that if the analyst can contain his "talion" response – the desire to retaliate in reenactment of the patient's negative internal object – he can break the pathological historic pattern. He does this by never retaliating and by recognizing the "complementary" countertransference he has been placed in (Lambert, 1972, p. 321). This has something to do with maintaining empathy, or struggling to, at all times.

In a later paper Lambert (1976) outlines five types of "counter-resistance" the analyst may perceive in himself. He again follows Racker and notes subjective experiences in which the analyst may feel angry, vengeful, verbally stuck, or fearful of the patient's negative response to or judgment of a premature interpretation.

THE BERLIN SCHOOL

The "Berlin" school of countertransference hardly exists as a school per se, consisting as it does of four analysts, three articles (translated into English) and two authors. However, a significant step toward a precise focus on the analyst has been made by them.

Dieckmann's presentation in 1971 to the Fifth International Jungian Congress marks the first in-depth reporting of the analyst's inner experience in analysis. He initially notes that the "full implications" of the dialectical relationship espoused by Jung have not yet been realized. Instead, even amongst Jungians, the focus of attention has been on patient rather than analyst (Dieckmann, 1974, p. 69).

As a corrective, Dieckmann and three other German analysts participated in a research project in which they recorded (and processed in a collegial group) their own associations to particular patient material. Their own associative content fell into four categories: 1) associations to the patient and in-session themes, 2) the analyst's own history and problems, 3) purely emotional reactions, and 4) physical responses.

The results, other than the above categorization, indicated to Dieckmann that there was a remarkably close "psychological connection between the analyst's chains of association and the patient's" (Dieckmann, 1974, p. 73). Phenomenologically, this took the form of the patient's often saying almost exactly what was on the analyst's mind[6]. Dieckmann goes on to give vivid examples showing either parallel or compensatory chains of mutual association, the first really self-revealing case examples since Jung's own (Jung, 1937, p. 332)[7].

Of interest technically is the Berlin group's emphasis on the initial difficulty but gradual ease of following one's own associations. Dieckmann adds most importantly that, even though countertransference-based interpretations were not given, the entire process seemed to be "guided" for both participants (Dieckmann, 1974, p. 75). Thus, interpretation seems to take a back seat to experience – if the analyst can get it right, so to speak, then it gets right in the patient *without its being said*. This silent but parallel tracking process "sounds mystical," says Dieckmann (p. 78), and in a way it is. He sees it as an ESP-analogous or Self-based phenomenon which is fundamentally *synchronistic*. Therefore, a cause and effect format, even such as projective identification, cannot account fully for countertransference/transference interactions.

Dieckmann's work is followed by an in-depth illustration by Blomeyer (1974). His presentation, even more self-disclosive than Dieckmann's, traces his countertransference from its original appearance as the "animal" appeal of a patient. Blomeyer also gives an example of how the analyst's experiential and even physical reality can be "reproduced" in the patient's dreams and in-session talk (Blomeyer, 1974, p. 107).

In a later paper Dieckmann (1976) synopsizes his research data, now gleaned from fifteen analysts over three years. The Self is postulated to synchronistically organize a virtually "complete correspondence" between analyst–patient associations, and this parallel process holds true even for very personal, non-archetypal analyst material (Dieckmann, 1976, pp. 26, 32). The prime focus of the research had been on archetypal dreams, and synchronicities were found to arise there especially. Associations to the analyst supervision group also occurred, which means to Dieckmann that the Self's sphere of influence extends still farther, into *unus mundus* areas.

However, just as the analyst's psyche links positively to the patient's, it may also resist it. The scope and power of this Self-guided process are perhaps what cause Dieckmann to suggest also that resistance is a *mutual* issue, "notwithstanding the [analyst's] training and experience" (Dieckmann, 1976, p. 27).

This Berlin conception does indeed have heavy implications – including some sort of defeat for the analyst's ego. Jung's statements about the analyst's "genuine participation, going right beyond professional routine . . . to the limits of his subjective possibilities" (Jung, 1946, p. 199) and his preference for a "mild" transference due to the "ordeal" involved (Jung, 1951a, p. 116) seem relevant here. Dieckmann's picture seems in that sense a little rosy, for the mutual chains of association will be not only wondrous but anxiety-provoking when they descend into darker areas.

Dieckmann concludes by citing four levels of the process. The first is *projective*, that is, illusory in the usual sense. The second is *objective* and, similar to Jung's "objective level" of interpretation, this level invites the analyst to particularly attend to his dreams about the patient. The third is the *antithetical* type of analytic interaction, where oppositional or complementary poles and roles are constellated. Finally, there is the *archetypal* situation, which, to be effective, requires that the archetype be "brought to life in the form of countertransference" – only then will it be facilitating to the patient (Dieckmann, 1976, p. 35).

All in all, the work of Dieckmann and the Berlin group gives new meaning and depth to the "Rainmaker" idea that Jung appeared to be fond of[8]. It brings this notion into the actual practice of analysis. In his first, 1974 paper Dieckmann alludes to this, as he tries to find a "middle way" somewhere between the introspective Rainmaker attitude and a more extraverted, "blank screen" attitude focussed primarily on the patient (Dieckmann, 1974, p. 71). Technically, he found it difficult to have one eye turned out and one in, so to speak. The split is resolved, however, by the synchronistic evidence presented, such that the analyst's inward focus turns out to flow in intimate conjunction with the patient's; hence it is not an empathic failure. In this model then, the *Tao* which organized the situation in the rainless Chinese village now orders the seemingly private, meditative processes of both analyst and patient.

THE "WOUNDED HEALER" SCHOOL

A "Wounded Healer" school of countertransference does not exist as such any more than a "Berlin" school exists. As defined here, the wounded healers consist of two Jungians, a Swiss and a American, who have picked up on Jung's references to the Greek myth of Asklepios and written about it with specific reference to its countertransference dimensions[9].

In an early article, "The Psychotherapist's Shadow" (1968), Guggenbuhl-Craig lays the groundwork for later study. Puncturing therapeutic omnipotence, he reminds us that analysis and all its Jungian concomitants (individuation, greater consciousness, etc.) "solve nothing and save no one" (Gugggenbuhl-Craig, 1968, p. 257). We cannot even measure, much less prove in a scientific manner, the things we believe in[10]. He then suggests that alongside the image of the benevolent doctor is that of the "charlatan, quack and false prophet" (p. 250).

In a minor confession Guggenbuhl reveals a patient's dream in which he (the analyst) was portrayed as a charlatan. This was initially interpreted as the patient's resistance; only later did Guggenbuhl-Craig see this as having objective possibilities. He goes on to note the paradoxical "tragedy" of being an analyst – greater areas of consciousness and individuation yield greater, more vivid areas of unconsciousness (Guggenbuhl-Craig, 1968, p. 251). The countertransference shadow of analysis is then delineated in detail: vicarious living via patients, jealous attacks on their spouses, protective diagnoses, spiritual inflation and philosophical arrogance. This is a good outline of some neurotic countertransference potentialities.

Continuing to shake us out of complacency, Guggenbuhl-Craig develops this topic in greater depth in his book, *Power in the Helping Professions* (1971). Taking off from earlier shadow themes, he notes how potent can be the analyst's fantasies, positive or negative, toward the patient. Since they have all the power of an active imagination, they may determine sickness and health. In other words, he is saying what Jung said, only in reverse: that the analyst's unconscious (or conscious) projections have an "inductive" effect on the patient.

Guggenbuhl-Craig ties in the above with consideration of what he postulates is a "healer-patient" archetype (Guggenbuhl-Craig, 1971, p. 85). People in the helping professions have a particular fascination with this bipolar archetype, he believes, but there is danger if the sickness side of it is left entirely with the patient. This is where the "charlatan" and shadow aspects can come into play – the analyst can lose awareness of the patient pole within himself and project it entirely onto the patient[11]. Similarly the patient may project his own "intra-psychic healer" or "healing factor" onto the analyst's persona (p. 90). Therefore, although both projections are appropriate and even understandable, Guggenbuhl-Craig feels a shift needs to happen whereby the archetype is not split between participants. For this to occur, the analyst clearly must be aware of the shadow side Guggenbuhl-Craig alludes to, internalize his own "wounded" pole, and realize like "the Greek physician, [that] only the divine healer can help ... the human doctor merely can facilitate its appearance" (p. 96).

Jess Groesbeck takes up Guggenbuhl-Craig's perspective and shows how actual wounded healing may take place. Drawing on the "like cures like" healing in homeopathy, Asklepian "incubation," the myth of the incurably wounded healer Chiron, and Jung's own physician, Groesbeck points out twin aspects of the process. One is the withdrawal of the mutual projections that take place at the persona level – i.e. "patient" and "doctor." The other is the development of the "inner healer" aspect within the patient.

25

This latter development, which is key, is facilitated in turn by two happenings. The patient's illness must activate the "personal wounds" and/or the wounded-healer archetype within the analyst. At this point, in order to help the patient "the analyst must show him the way," by experiencing the archetype and its personal ramifications himself (Groesbeck, 1975, p. 132). Thus the analyst is simultaneously a "guide," a participatory role model and a catalyst for the patient's "inner healer" (p. 130).

Due to the very necessary and personal inner aspect of all this for the analyst, Groesbeck suggests that there are analysts who are thus "constantly being analyzed and illumined by their patients" (Groesbeck, 1975, p. 133). For such "wounded healers" there are two dangers to watch out for: inflation and death. Realizing that the personal involvement and healing processes are archetypally based can help deflate the over-zealous or over-whelmed analyst. This recalls Jung's "deo concedente" (Jung, 1946, p. 190) maxim, as well as Guggenbuhl-Craig's note above about human reliance upon the "divine healer."

Groesbeck articulates the healing process with a series of complex diagrams somewhat similar to Jung's "adept-soror" diagram in "The Psychology of the Transference" (Jung, 1946, p. 221). In this case however, Groesbeck shows various permutations involving connection with the underlying "wounded healer" archetype. His case examples also neatly show the evolving growth of patients' inner healers as imaged in dreams. Though he does not refer much to the possibly objective aspects of these dreams of the analyst, Groesbeck does show the analyst's gradual "psychic infection" through some psychophysical reactions and parallel dreams. The latter is reminiscent of some of the Dieckmann research.

Groesbeck concludes from all this that training analysis and a periodic post-training return to analysis are important. The main thrust of his paper, though, is upon the "here and now," in-session countertransference (re)wounding that occurs. He closes his ground-breaking paper with some of his own dreams, which suggest the importance of the fact that "in analytical work one cannot hide wounds or weaknesses" (Groesbeck, 1975, p. 143).

THE LANGSIAN GROUP

In terms of Jungian approaches to countertransference, the 1980s opened with a bang. William Goodheart spearheaded a some-what controversial effort to bring the psychoanalytic theories of Robert Langs into Jungian circles. While Langs' work is extensive and not all of it pertinent to this book, several key features, as understood by Goodheart, are relevant.

For Goodheart, Langs' central contribution lies in showing how the patient's unconscious will in effect make "creative efforts" to orient the analyst properly during analytic sessions (Goodheart, 1980, p. 2). A special style of sequential listening is required, in which the analyst notes the manifest content of associ-ations and understands these as unconscious commentaries on the analyst's prior intervention or behavior. The patient and analyst thus engage in a continuous interaction which can be monitored by the analyst consciously (and monitored unconsciously by the patient's associations).

Goodheart bases his Langsian synthesis on Jung's theory that analysis is a "dialectical" process, only Goodheart gives this a special twist such that "nothing happens in a therapeutic hour within the patient or therapist which is not an interactional product" (Goodheart, 1984, pp. 90–91). Patients are thus making, via their associations, not only intrapsychic statements but specific responses to the analyst's comments and activities. The activities implicitly reacted to are not just the most recent inter-vention, but especially the analyst's attempts or agreements to modify the ground rules of analysis – the analytic frame.

It is in this area that Goodheart sees much opportunity for acting out by the analyst. Whether instigated by patient or analyst, the alteration of the stable container of analysis is an attempt to relieve rather than confront and understand a difficult emotional state. What happens typically is that the patient will request some concrete gratification as a defense against his conflicts. Instead of bearing with his own anxiety – the "analytic strain" – the analyst knuckles under and abandons the analytic attitude (Goodheart, 1984, p. 98). He has therefore succumbed to a neurotic counter-transference.

In this "seamlessly interpenetrating" interchange between analyst and patient, the patient will be monitoring the analyst quite closely in this quasi-supervisory, even quasi-therapeutic way (Goodheart, 1985, p. 161). The patient will even produce images "best viewed as highly cogent unconscious efforts to conduct a therapy on the therapist" when the latter is way off

27

(Goodheart, 1984, p. 106). For example, the client might produce imagery of the kind of analyst or analyst response that is required. Goodheart, utilizing Langs' theories, suggests that the analyst should not just take the patient's compliance as an affirmation, but listen for the subsequent, positive or negative associations which will tell the real story.

Within Goodheart's model, then, the analyst's shadow comes under constant surveillance. Analytic and personal integrity are required to undergo this very specific application of Jung's theory of "objective" interpretation. In this instance, the manifest content of client associations, fantasies and dreams is referred to analyst interventions on a microscopic level. This is a variation on the traditional psychoanalytic idea that all client material in a session is transference-oriented, that it all refers to the analyst. Here, however, it is the analyst's actual shadow, not the analyst as transference figure that is the center of attention.

Goodheart's is a method for detecting countertransference. He has given us a technique for self-monitoring. There are echoes of the London idea that the analyst can adapt to meet the patient's needs. However, it is not a model that relies on countertransference per se as an "organ of information." The *patient's* unconscious is the perceptual organ. The type of countertransference Goodheart is talking about is basically the "neurotic" or "illusory" type. He states this clearly when he contends that following his technique will compel the analyst to face "the experience of the patient's continuously outlining the most conflict laden and personally painful weaknesses of the therapist" (Goodheart, 1984, p. 107).

Goodheart's work has received both criticism and support from Jungian analysts (see Kugler and Hillman, 1985). An article by Parks (1987) offers some vivid personal examples which help illustrate the technique. She candidly describes several "therapeutic misalliances" she falls into but then corrects; the fact of her countertransferences is revealed, though the working through of the countertransference is not.

For instance, Parks (1987, p. 106) asks herself, regarding an "interest-free loan" to a patient, "Why had I done it in the first place?" – but doesn't answer the question (in print, at least)[12]. She does however re-modify the frame appropriately. We see here, as with most Langs–Goodheart examples, that recognition and containment of "shadow" are generally considered sufficient.

Another issue vis-a-vis Goodheart that Parks answers is where to *place* the interpretative leverage – objectively or subjectively? Clearly the patient's "supervisory" associations are subjective reactions to objective analyst failures. As Parks puts it, she prefers "considering the therapist's misunderstandings and misinterpretations before considering the patient's distortions" (Parks, 1987, p. 111). Thus the standard operating procedure around the analyst's viewpoint on projection is radically shifted. Indeed it is not quite clear, to this author, what exactly is the status of the "internal" within the Goodheartian frame. Though he postulates an "intrapsychic life" (Goodheart, 1984, p. 91) and a "secured-symbolizing field" (Goodheart, 1980, p. 4), movement to the intrapsychic, if any, is not much contemplated in the examples. When, if at all, are deduced client "commentaries" on the analyst's shadow taken subjectively, transferentially or even historically? Is there a point at which interpretations shift, or should? Perhaps it is the case that answers to these questions have not been arrived at yet. Meanwhile, Goodheart's method is a valuable addition to a clinical approach.

JACOBY'S APPROACH

The work on countertransference by Mario Jacoby is important in many ways, including that he is a Zurich analyst who has a developmental outlook and that he wrote the first post-Jungian book (1984) on transference/countertransference.

His first published thoughts on the issue, however, were in a 1971 article on transference. In it he describes an important dream from a deprived, self-deprecating patient. Among other things the dream touched on Jacoby's own interests in an uncanny way. He further describes the patient's obvious importance to him and his own self-questioning: since this patient needed "total commitment" from him, he wondered, "Am I prepared for that?" Apparently so, because he goes on to say, "On the basis of various experiences of my own that resembled hers, I concluded that her fate had gotten very under my skin" (Jacoby, 1971, p. 15). Thus he gives a pretty good example, in similar terms, of Jung's ideas about the analyst's accepting as destiny his own tendency to be psychically infected: "The patient then means something to him personally, and this provides the most favourable basis for treatment" (Jung, 1946, p. 177). Jacoby does not go on to describe further the particular, mutual resemblances and how he worked with them, though.

In his book of lectures (1984) Jacoby sets out to describe the analyst–patient relationship in simple, feeling terms rather than in a scholarly, experience-distant fashion. His examples show a free range of countertransference experiences and reactive possibilities. For instance, a patient dreams that Jacoby lends her a relevant book by Jung, so he actually does so. Yet Jacoby is aware of the potential complications of this "acting out," so he follows up on it, exploring their interactive process and at least three transference positions he may possibly have "incarnated" for her (Jacoby, 1984, p. 21). Another patient (the same one as in the 1971 paper, above) dreams a dream that so moves him and impresses on him their fusion that "somehow it could have been a dream of my own in connection with the patient . . . . As a matter of fact, the dream really belonged to us both" (p. 33). Without so describing it, Jacoby here has described a provocative new way of looking at the dream in close analytic interactions.

Turning to countertransference as such, Jacoby outlines how it can be used to "uncover unconscious dynamics going on in the patient" (Jacoby, 1984, p. 37). With good examples he describes the syntonic/concordant/complementary possibilities primarily synthesized by the London school. What is striking, again, is his demonstration of a finely tuned feeling function and a fluid openness to alternative explanations. What is new is his suggestion that illusory and syntonic transferences typically are *mixed*[13]. The "either-or" concept, where countertransference is strictly neurotic *or* informational, is in this way relativized.

Jacoby's attention also turns to the work of Heinz Kohut, showing various countertransference reactions taking place within Kohut's "selfobject" framework. He points out with subtlety the experience and reactions to "mirror" transferences in which the analyst may feel either used or vital to the patient. In these complex selfobject positions, where sensitive response and "empathic resonance" are narcissistically demanded, Jacoby nevertheless warns against making "empty, routine interventions" (Jacoby, 1984, p. 49), i.e. ones that seem empathic but really aren't. He provides good examples of how analytic integrity, combined with honesty, can pave a better way toward resolution of the mirror transference. He is similarly revealing and astute about the "idealizing" transference and its accompanying countertransference. In these selfobject states, says Jacoby, the analyst is embodying archetypal projections of the patient's, and not always in their positive forms. Sometimes the Self may be what is being idealized. The archetypal element in these selfobject fusions can also lead to questions of illusional vs. delusional transference. Except in purely psychotic states, Jacoby sees a "sliding scale" here (p. 56), just as he sees oscillation between mirror and idealizing transferences. And much as the "as if" aspect of the patient's projection and "use" of the analyst varies, so the analyst's countertransference can sometimes veer into the more delusional realm (p. 58). Jacoby gives an excellent example of his own loss of the "as if" standpoint, followed by his own projection of the "grandiose self" onto his patient, which is in turn followed by Jacoby's recovery of analytic stance.

Here, as before, Jacoby's revealing and personable style are evident. He provides guidelines for ways to reach and reach out to patients. In a more recent article this is literally the case, as he describes the occasions, albeit rare, when his concordant fantasies allow him to empathically hold a patient's hand at critical moments. Referring to his countertransference experience of the "crying child" within patients, Jacoby (1986, p. 122) shows us gentle touches, cautiously considered and movingly described.

SCHWARTZ-SALANT'S WORK

Nathan Schwartz-Salant's extensive work during the 1980s follows naturally upon Jacoby's. Both are influenced by and make Jungian syntheses of Kohut's work. Schwartz-Salant, however, in his book on narcissism (1982) presents a more detailed clinical picture when elucidating the effects of mirror and idealizing merger transferences on the analyst. He makes extremely precise differentiations about how to work with them, based on his vision of the archetypal processes involved.

In general, whereas Jacoby presents a clearer, often more understandable picture, Schwartz-Salant presents a heavily amplified one. The latter's is a very personal vision – not that all theories aren't – but one that requires a good deal of commitment to understanding it. This is partly because Schwartz-Salant is creating a more complex model. Delusional transference/counter-transference states, which Jacoby enters into but has hesitations about, seem to lie at the core of Schwartz-Salant's theory.

This difference in degree may be best expressed in their respective ideas of what analysis "is." Jacoby calls it two people trying "to understand what is going on in the unconscious of *one* of them" (Jacoby, 1984, p. 13, my emphasis). Of course, Jacoby makes and shows much use of his own unconscious in the process. Schwartz-Salant on the other hand says analysis is "a strange endeavor of two people *mutually* constellating the unconscious" (Schwartz-Salant, 1984, p. 29, my emphasis). Of course, he is directing attention ultimately towards the patient's cure. Both would probably agree with each other, yet the difference in words and focus may be relevant.

While much of Schwartz-Salant's work takes form in his first book, in subsequent works he really crystallizes his ideas on the nature of countertransference and the analytic interaction. To a greater extent than any of the previously mentioned authors, he takes Jung's alchemical metaphor, uses it directly and extends it. Others tend to modify Jung's diagrams from "The Psychology of the Transference"; Schwartz-Salant actually takes the Rosarium images and utilizes them in explicating his theory of "imaginal" spaces, "subtle body" concepts and "inner couples" as applied to the transference/countertransference process.

While being thoroughly versed in "the developmental perspective" and often making use of it, Schwartz-Salant fundamentally feels that it "falters" in explaining modes of deep analyst–patient experience (Schwartz-Salant, 1988a, p. 1). In order to understand the archetypal energies envisioned in *coniunctio* imagery, a more "imaginal" type of model, beyond projective and introjective identification, is needed.

According to Schwartz-Salant a "shared imaginal realm," based on quasi-concrete energy fields historically known as the "subtle body," may exist in a kind of psychic space between patient and analyst (Schwartz-Salant, 1986, p. 24). This is not a literally seen space, but a definitely felt, aura-like "field" that is mutually imagined. This is something like active imagination, except that two people are involved. Schwartz-Salant notes that it is neither here nor there, in nor out, but is "other:" it is "in between" the two participants but not really in any place per se, more in an "imaginal world" (Schwartz-Salant, 1988b, p. 43). Clearly, the standard paradigms of space/time and causality are altered here; hence its linkage with the unconscious as Jung sees it – an archetypal, acausal, fourth-dimensional and religious realm (Schwartz-Salant, 1990, p. 145).

The interactions that take place in this field are what the alchemical pictures show. Often the field or the analyst's experience will indicate the existence of a "couple," like the king and queen in the alchemical pictures, in various states of conjunction, depression, incestuous embrace and so on. While the original, pathological nature of the coupling may be formed out of early personal experience of parents, the healing that may take place is the result of a shared, archetypal process.

Within this highly complex rubric Schwartz-Salant outlines many dimensions of countertransference. It is rather difficult, yet necessary here, to discuss them out of context. Much of his theory and approach were developed from work with borderline patients, with whom he cites a vast range of emotions: fear, hate, self-hatred, helplessness, inauthenticity *and* empathy, to name just a few. It is out of his understanding of such reactions (via the archetypal, subtle body and coupling perspectives above) that empathy and further participation in the alchemical process are maintained. This is somewhat similar, though the explanatory basis is different, to the transformations of less savory counter-transferences into syntonic ones that other Jungians describe.

There are several technical aspects of Schwartz-Salant's work that stand out. His basic viewpoint, of course, is a central feature and is more archetypal, mutual and mystical than that of most countertransference writers, who tend to stress the personal. His writing style also conveys a sense of an unusual level of engagement with his patients. The emphasis on imaginal sight is unique, yet it is interestingly based on a bodily felt relationship to the psyche, patient and their shared space. A temporary sacrifice of the same intellect which Schwartz-Salant so vividly demonstrates in his numerous writings is involved. He speaks too of "sacrificing interpretations" in order that the pre-verbal, interactive field may be opened up and entered (Schwartz-Salant, 1988b, p. 51; 1989, p. 109). In these sometimes psychotic areas, only the imagination can serve as a true guide. Vis-à-vis the question of self-disclosure, Schwartz-Salant is radical, as his theory naturally demands. In addition, he repeatedly insists on the validation of patient's accurate intuitive perceptions of the analyst. Otherwise, especially in borderline patients, this crucial and potent "psychic

33

organ" – the patient's truthful though painful vision – may again be split off (1988a, p. 16).

In his most recent article Schwartz-Salant breaks new ground by fully elucidating his psychotic countertransference and its incestuous roots in the Attis–Cybele, "son-lover" archetype. He goes farther than he has before in showing his struggles, resistances and ultimate honesty. Thus, he notes, "Imaginal sight will only be available to us when we consciously see through the eyes of our own complexes" (Schwartz-Salant, 1990, p. 154).

Schwartz-Salant's is a sometimes difficult vision. Words do not do it justice – and that is perhaps a problem. It is a highly personalized theory with his own, specialized language. Of course, Jung's alchemical-transference treatise can be obscure as well. Schwartz-Salant brings "Psychology of the Transference" down to earth in many ways, but not completely and not easily. Then too the Self and the whole *"Mysterium Coniunctionis"* is just that, a mystery. He echoes Dieckmann when he (Schwartz-Salant) suggests that causal theories won't quite fit the facts and that the deeper unconscious is only fully constellated via the countertransference (Dieckmann, 1974, 1976). He sounds like Jacoby (see p. 30, above) when he describes the analytic interaction as "a mutual dream . . . being dreamed" (Schwartz-Salant, 1988b, p. 50).

In conclusion, Schwartz-Salant builds from a basic model of projective identification and takes off from there into a new interactive realm. For some, it may be difficult to follow him there. Reminiscent of Jung's (1977, p. 428) "I don't need to believe, I know" comments on religious experience, Schwartz-Salant states, "we are concerned not with ordinary perceptions, but with imaginal ones. Those who can *see* will do so; others will remain skeptical" (Schwartz-Salant, 1986, p. 21).

INTO THE 1990s

Some contributions by other authors, particularly Samuels (1985, 1989, 1993) and Steinberg (1989) carry this countertransference review into the 1990s. Like other Jungians reviewed here, Samuels (1989) provides some new ways of looking at *imagery* that are relevant to analytic interaction. As opposed to Goodheart, who links images with objective countertransference issues, Samuels suggests a "metaphorical" approach in which parental images in particular can reflect the patient's own self-parenting, self-therapeutic or potentially integratable shadow qualities (Samuels, 1989, p. 48). Of interest here technically is that Samuels, unlike Schwartz-Salant for instance, downplays the personal vs. archetypal question in favor of an image-based strategy. Everything can be metaphor, and it needn't be numinous or archetypal to be potent. Within Samuels' "pluralistic" point of view, historical facts can also be heard as metaphors or as "self-monitoring" or "self-diagnostic" statements (p. 50).

This imagistic background is relevant for moving directly into Samuels' countertransference ideas. Playing off Freud's words, Samuels states that "the analyst's inner world . . . is the *via regia* into the inner world of the patient" (Samuels, 1985, p. 51). Two types of usable countertransferences are offered: 1) the *reflective*, where the analyst's feelings closely reflect the patient's unconscious inner state and 2) the *embodied*, where the analyst feels like a particular "person" (i.e. a "complex," internal object or object representation) who inhabits the patient's inner world (p. 52).

While noting that this typology overlaps to some degree with those of Fordham and Racker, Samuels feels his new words are better descriptors of the actual experience of the analyst. The body reference is especially important, as the patient's problem or state really gets "embodied" in the analyst, who feels it in his body. To test this, Samuels created a small research project and found three classes of countertransference responses (all of which he also regards as "images"): body/behavioral, feelings and fantasies. His theory leads to the subtle idea not only of embodying countertransference, but through embodiment being able to "augment" the unconscious issue when returning it, slightly reshaped and highlighted as it were, to the patient (Samuels, 1989, p. 159).

The context for all this, particularly the bodily-experienced "visions" the analyst may feel, is not just himself or the patient but a "shared *mundus imaginalis*" (Samuels, 1985, p. 59). This idea and its body basis were developed somewhat later and in different terms by Schwartz-Salant (1986; see pp. 32–34). Samuels notes, however, that there are important differences. In his approach the analyst prefers to wait for countertransference rather than actively "quest for imaginal sight;" second, Samuels feels that Schwartz-Salant over-"couples" things (Samuels, 1989, p. 172).

In 1985 Samuels also, in the course of attempting to answer to the analytic mainstream "What on earth?" Jung was doing when using alchemy to explain transference, suggests that analytic participants are in effect "analytically married" (Samuels, 1989, pp. 176, 185). Hence the alchemical *hierosgamos* ("sacred marriage") imagery makes sense. Though he does not specify the exact countertransference implications, Samuels' discussion of higher/ lower dimensions of the eros concept is no doubt relevant. Lest Jungians fly too high, he notes, "Sexuality has to be present for its symbolic meaning to be interpreted . . . . no eros, no analysis" (Samuels, 1989, pp. 187, 190). In terms of current countertransference interest, there can be little question that eros in all its complexity (sexual, spiritual, incestuous, sublimated, related, "kinship libido" connected, "heart-centered," or whatever) is paramount.

Samuels (1993) continues his countertransference work in a more recent book which extends clinical ideas into the broader field of politics. He does not analyze politics along countertransference/transference dimensions (as might be expected); rather, Samuels suggests the application and appreciation of the subjective point of view in political discourse. Along the way, he offers, again, a very lucid review of countertransference developments over time, as well as an effective epistemological critique of "projective identification."

This literature review ends with Warren Steinberg's (1989) article in which he stresses the need for more elaboration of the countertransference process per se. Accordingly, his work features good examples and finely tuned pointers. For instance, in overcoming analyst resistance to a spontaneous countertransference fantasy, he suggests it is important to separate the themes from the actual imagery. This is so because contents clothed in his own imagery rather than the patient's tend to feel more threatening to the analyst (Steinberg, 1989, p. 13). Focusing on the theme itself neutralizes the fear and the possible over-responsibility.

Steinberg classifies countertransference in usual ways – useful, neurotic, erotic and archetypal. Some of his sub-types, though, are new in the Jungian literature and benefit from psychoanalytic views. For instance, the "neurotic" form can be subdivided into *characterological* and *acute* (from Reich and Langs). He also points out that introjective identification can be defensively misused as a rationalization for a stuck analyst. Harold Searles' work is brought into play in support of a new notion – that even the neurotic countertransference in itself can lead to helpful information. This is a "combination" viewpoint, with the analyst's neurotic parts linked with projected patient roles (Steinberg, 1989, p. 19). Previous authors have tended to suggest a more distinct sequence from neurotic to syntonic.

Like Samuels, Steinberg presents a differentiated view of eros, specifically of the erotic countertransference. He has doubts about Jung's idea that it compensates poor rapport. Erotic reactions present multiple possibilities: from repression and deprivation in either party to seduction, first growth, characterological disturbance or *coniunctio* energy. Finally, Steinberg gives examples of how to deal with archetypal identifications/inflations – by deflating them through amplification and a good sense of humor.

To make these delicate differentiations, Steinberg suggests some safeguards for the analyst: 1) self-knowledge in general, 2) checking whether the subjective fantasy is unusual for him or not, and 3) noticing the level or type of affect when intervening. In other words, the analyst should note both *how* he is interpreting and *where* he is interpreting from.

37

3

CASE ILLUSTRATIONS

As the previous chapter indicated, countertransference discussions generally show the finished products rather than the ways and means of working with countertransference. The actual phenomenology of the countertransference – what the experience is really "like," what is happening "in" the analyst and how it evolves – receives less attention. Yet Jung and his recent followers stress the importance of this dimension of Jungian clinical practice and directly or implicitly call for some real explication of it. The purpose of this chapter is to illustrate how the analyst actually wrestles with his reactions or wounds.

The analyst here is the author. The material is taken from the first two years of supervised work with two very different analysands while the author was an analyst-in-training. This training facet colored the countertransference situation, as will be seen, but also gave further impetus to the author's efforts at self-scrutiny. Furthermore, the training dimension encouraged then and permits now the use of detailed notes taken at the time. The patient and countertransference material presented here are taken verbatim (with slight modifications for style) from these case or personal notes, though the discussion of the content may include present as well as past reflections.

The nature of this material and the training context will invite interpretation of the countertransference and discussion of technique. While that discussion is inevitable, it is perhaps not the most beneficial way to approach this material. This chapter consists of selected contents, from a vast array of material in each analysis, chosen with an eye on countertransference issues in particular. A large amount of analytic data – dreams, fantasies, in- and out-of-session events, memories, history, interpretations and reflections on all these – is left out. While this other material helps form the overall fabric of the analysis, it would be impossible to present it all. Transcripts alone of psychotherapy sessions are usually quite tedious, and the examples here seek to add other, unseen but crucial, dimensions. So a full-scale presentation is not feasible, as in all case presentations.

Even the selected countertransference material itself is copious, especially in the first case here. Again, the emphasis upon it is not meant to devalue other approaches, issues or styles. The greater danger is typically in the opposite direction – that countertransference may be feared, ignored and/or undervalued.

A countertransference-based style of working involves more than the periodic or occasionally required glance at one's internal processes. Rather, it is a slow, continuous process. In my experience this ongoing work with the countertransference often synchronizes with or parallels the patient's own internal developments. In other words, the analyst is organically linked with the patient's unconscious. The examples here are meant to show or at least suggest the intricacies of this complex interaction.

This chapter's format borrows from some more detailed Jungian case studies, especially "Individual Dream Symbolism in Relation to Alchemy" (Jung, 1936), and Adler's lengthy case in *The Living Symbol* (1961). These studies show symbolic (primarily dream) movements over a period of time. The examples in this chapter will add the countertransference factor to this layout and discuss the analyst's subjective experience in conjunction with certain of the patient's material. The sequences occurred in the order they occurred, although time foci here are irregular. That is, the camera sometimes focusses very minutely on material a few seconds apart, sometimes on material months apart and of a different type.

"Countertransference" can be defined narrowly or liberally (see Kernberg, 1965). The material here accords with the "total" response school, where all inner or outer processes in relation to the patient *can* be relevant. The breadth, depth or even looseness of countertransference reactions do not necessarily imply anything about their disclosure to the patient (never say "never," but this author does not reveal dreams or countertransference conflicts per se to patients). At any rate, the material here will include a wide range of in-session and out-of-session fantasies, feelings, dreams and speculations about patients and others.

Determinations about countertransference pathology are also frequent: is the analyst's experience "neurotic" or even "psychotic" in a particular instance? This can (and should) be part of the ongoing countertransference struggle, as the examples will show. There is little doubt that the countertransferences here are often "mine" or "neurotic." However, there is no doubt either that ideas about the "wounded healer" and "a good half" of analysis being the analyst's self-analysis must have some real body to them (or else are meaningless or frivolous). A wounded healer without a wound and a self-analysis without the real self are pointless. The concluding chapter will speak more to these and other issues that the case presentations raise.

Extensive patient histories, though important, are not possible here for confidentiality reasons. In what follows there are certain allusions to personal history that have been modified or disguised in an attempt to preserve a relatively accurate representation of their historical relevance to the treatment.

CASE ONE: MS. F

F was the daughter of a once severely alcoholic mother and a father who was a well-known man in certain circles. The parents divorced before F entered her teen years. Her adolescence was also stormy, involving considerable serious drug activity and acting out. At one point F had been sent away to school and then to a psychiatric hospital (which she described as a "country club"). Following that she ran away with a boyfriend, and continued to live in a countercultural style she still valued. A creative individual from a cultured background, she ultimately married a man whom she had worked with artistically. F was a working mother, who presented with marital, family and sexual concerns as well as Jungian interests.

Course of treatment and countertransference

1.

Patient	*Countertransference*
About a year before actually entering analysis, F called to inquire about an appointment.	I was eager for new clients and hoped to sign her up.

She then launched into a description of a deeply felt, quasi-transcendent, "nature" experience.	I was uncomfortable with this "instant" phone intimacy and couldn't get with what she was talking about, though it sounded important to her.
F then asked, "What do you think about that?"	Actually, I thought she sounded pretty "spacey" – a flower child? Wanting a new client, I tried to respond with something relevant.
[An appointment was set up which she later cancelled or did not show up for.]	My image of her (or the failure of my answer) seemed confirmed.

Discussion

Much is going on in analysis even before the first analytic hour. The analyst is immediately giving and getting impressions; he needs to be ready to work. As Jung notes in terms of the transference, "Often it is in full swing before he [the analyst] has even opened his mouth" (Jung, 1946, p. 171n). This is equally true for the countertransference. Already I had a personal agenda that, however understandable, colored my responses – new patients. Already I had begun to form an image ("flower child") of this unseen patient. Already, perhaps, I had flunked her first test of me.

These early images, in both directions between analyst and patient, have an almost tangible quality to them (a "feeling" as well as a visual image) and might be called "feeling images."[1] They are subject to pre-existing transferences and countertransferences. From the therapist's perspective, there is a readiness to imagine and feel a patient, perhaps like a mother expecting a child. The "idea" of a patient, which starts to be filled in by introjections and projections, then adjusts and moves over time.

2.

Patient

[Some months later, at a showing of some Jungian movies, I noticed this very attractive, dark-haired woman at the end of my row.]

Countertransference

I had a fleeting fantasy of having an affair with this beautiful, Jungian-oriented female.

41

During the audience discussion she said she had briefly visited the Jung Institute.

More interesting still. At a younger age I had made a lengthy pilgrimage to Zurich.

Discussion

Not just the patient but the *therapist* brings his entire "self" – neuroses, wounds, needs, soul, etc. – to the analysis. This in turn becomes part of the analyst–patient mix in which "both are transformed" (Jung, 1929a, p. 71). The theme of the "other woman" was one that cropped up with some frequency in my dream and fantasy life. This took the form of a rather conflicted yearning (as I was married and a father) to "fall in love." The other woman in the fantasy was often a creative or poetic type – sometimes a psychologist. Here we have someone who can fit the fantasy bill for me: an attractive, "psyche"-oriented, "anima" figure (in Jungian terms), who may even have gone on the same inner/outer quest I had.

3.

Patient	Countertransference
At the end of the final intermission, she approached me and introduced herself, noting we had talked before.	*I was undoubtedly pleased when this woman of my fantasy sought me out, and that we apparently knew each other . . .*
[Moving into a professional persona, I said, "Oh yes, perhaps we could talk briefly after the movie."]	*. . . but tried to act neutral.*
At the end she was not there.	*I was puzzled by this disappearing act, after the breathtaking fantasy she had inspired. I wondered again if she was kind of "spacey."*

Discussion

Thus a pre-analytic countertransference fantasy is, to repeat Jung's words, "in full swing." In this case there is a constellation of my needs and conflicts. In retrospect, my earlier, haughty critique of

F's longing for a quasi-transcendent "nature" experience was partly related to my own yearnings for the "mysteries" of romance. In that sense she was no more "spacey" or naive-sounding than I was. Her elusive quality and sudden disappearance may have fit the countertransference situation both archetypally (the mysterious anima) and personally (my own fleeting feelings and fantasies).

4.

Transference	*Countertransference*
Some months later F called again, at home. She said she had a new job with insurance coverage that would soon come into play.	*I was not unhappy she called. Phoning me at home felt overly intimate, but I had the number on my tape.*
She asked me: 1) if I ever reduced my fees, and 2) if I would see her now but postdate it for insurance purposes?	*As when F had first phoned, I felt pressured to answer important, loaded questions I was not ready to answer.*
[I replied that I had on occasion reduced my fees.]	*I did not want to reduce my fees but wanted this new patient for financial, training and perhaps "anima" reasons.*
[About the insurance I replied, "That would be fraudulent" and I therefore could not do it.]	*I was struck by the adamant quality of my refusal to commit "fraud" – I could have just said "no" politely.*

Discussion

The patient begins to "push" further into me and is met by some confused resistance. Even with (or perhaps especially with) a desirable client the mutual analytic "engagement" is quite taxing. So it usually takes time and a more definite commitment before I can let a patient "in." This is a boundary phenomenon. With this patient, however, I am already "constellated," so to speak. My almost self-righteous stand on insurance fraud was partly an effort to control my guilty fantasies about breaking the "law" with this attractive patient: I wanted to remind both of us that I was "all business."

But, while I was struggling with my vulnerability to a fantasy seduction, it was interesting that F had *immediately* asked for special treatment, even collusion. My moralistic tone was not only for self-control or "frame" reasons, but because she somehow pulled that right away. Though I didn't know it at the time, F needed someone "to do the right thing" on her behalf, or at least fill a patriarchal role.

All this was taking place before F had had one hour of actual analysis. Indeed, all of this discussion ideally should have taken place "in the hour." These nuances of neurotic/complementary countertransference, patient/therapist resistance, boundary penetration and container formation are dimly conceived at this point, yet they are entirely in operation.

5.

Transference	Countertransference
In our first session F said, "I'm in a lot of pain . . . I'm good at being strong or surviving, but I need a place like here not to be strong."	*I was impressed by her psychological-mindedness and openness here and throughout this initial meeting.*
She then mentioned ambivalent feelings about her father. She was angry at him but half-jokingly said, "Don't ask [about him] . . . Ask me something else . . . . I wish he'd call . . . . I need to leave."	*I wondered about an actual incest situation with her father.*
F next spoke of her longing for a "male deity" on an inner level.	*Would I figure into this fantasy? Could I? This had appeal for me.*
She spoke also of "a sexual thing with male friends . . . longing for love, approval, a narcissistic kind of feeling."	*Indeed. I wrote down simultaneously in my notes as I listened, "I feel a sexual pull towards her."*
She wanted to feel "special" and wondered if I'd been watching her out the window.	*I hadn't been (but I had noticed her from "afar" at the movie).*

44

She imagined but had no memory of incest with her father or eldest brother.	*Perhaps there had been incest.*
Money matters felt "sleazy, secretive and connected with father, like sex."	*When she linked money, sex and father, I wrote down in my notes, "Oedipal?"*
[F then asked for a fee reduction.]	*What to do?*
[I hedged, acknowledging F's financial concerns and asking a few pertinent questions. I suggested she make a budget so we could then look at the fee situation.]	*I was conflicted about the fee issue, wanting to maintain the correct stance for analysis rather than simply granting this needy, "appealing" woman her every wish.*

Discussion

The whole analytic relationship, from history to fees to countertransference, was heavily colored with incest issues from the very beginning. F moved speedily past any social taboos; of course my fantasies about her had moved right along too, to say the least. I was trying to hold the line on the analytic container and on my feelings. It was interesting how my "other woman" fantasies seemed to jibe in general with her "other man" fantasies (whether that man be a deity, friend or family member). These parallels in patient and therapist created potentials for a confusing, *incest-like* area of "mutual unconsciousness" and for spontaneous combustion in the analytic vessel.

6.

Transference	*Countertransference*
F gently but rather persistently complained that I had "promised" her a reduced fee.	*I kicked myself for in effect offering the option, if not "promise," of a reduction.*
When I asked instead what a fee change might mean to her, F said she would feel powerful and special, not "helpless" and somehow obligated to me.	*She already felt "special" to me — too special I thought. I was trying not to feel helpless and in her power.*

"I could leave," she also said with a laugh, "if you don't do it."

I hoped she wouldn't and doubted she would, but I felt a bit threatened. [However, since F could afford my fees, I decided not to reduce them.]

Discussion

I was still trying to recover here from my previous mistake of trying to "seduce" new patients, especially this one, into analysis. Unbeknownst to her perhaps, she had the "power" to toy with me to some extent ("I could leave"). In fact there was on her side some apparent flirtation going on and more unconscious pressure on me here to do the "wrong" thing. This was successfully resisted, as F's next dream seemed to indicate.

7. Patient's dream

Standing in front of the kitchen stove in the house I grew up in. A doctor is hugging me sideways with his arms around my waist. I felt proud and good.

Transference

F associated to the kitchen as "Mother's little place, Mother's element," where she used to be "in control, then in a [drunken] stupor."

The doctor was a kindly one she knew and with whom F felt "valued and central."

Countertransference

I silently associated to another dream, the first of the analysis: F was with mother in a hometown mall and a teenage psychiatric patient began to throw up everywhere.

I was glad the "doctor" (i.e. me) was imaged as not hugging her too sexually.

Discussion

A positive therapeutic "holding" and incest containment (acted out by us around the fee dilemma) seems to be confirmed in this dream coupling – intimate but safely non-sexual and entering into the narcissistically damaged mother area of childhood. The patient dreams of what she needs or what she's getting. The dream can provide not only an image of the patient's private, inner world, but of the analytic situation and countertransference as well. I chose to see this mainly as a commentary on my "frame" interventions (a "secondary derivative" in Langs' terminology). Furthermore, just as the vomiting adolescent might represent the "inner patient" in F's first dream, so perhaps the "inner healer" pole of Groesbeck's "Wounded Healer" archetype is portrayed by the doctor in this second one. The sideways embrace (and my asexual "relief") are interesting, however, hinting at the incestuous "left-hand" *coniunctio* connection in this early stage of the analysis (see Jung, 1946, p. 217).

8.

Transference	*Countertransference*
F described a number of "lost waif" dreams and her own hatred of the child within.	I wondered if I could help her, and was disturbed by her self-hatred.
A few days before, F had had an abortion but felt unsupported by her doctor and husband. She said she had called me but my answering machine was broken and cut her off.	I felt guilty and professionally inadequate about my apparent empathic failures with this so obviously wounded, "lost child" client.
In session she began to cry very quietly but I didn't see it. She told me she wanted me to "intervene" more.	I wanted to protest in my defense that she made her pain hard to see.
Further wish-fantasies: "Just you, your wife and me, no kids or other patients . . . Dad kidnapping me to show that he cared."	I worried, doubly guilty, that my erotic interest crippled my ability to give her the exclusive empathic attention that she desired.
F asked for more frequent sessions at a reduced fee.	On the spot about the fee, again.
[We looked at her finances and I agreed to let her run a bill for the added sessions until she could pay me in a couple of months.]	I felt a strong pull to repair my empathic failures, self-esteem and guilty conscience by granting her fee request.

Discussion

The pressure on the outer "frame" of analysis, fueled by outer and inner needs of both parties, was intense at this point. On the external level, it was realistically dealt with in a compromise formation – she required more sessions at a fee she could afford. F's protest about what Kohut (1971, 1977) might term "selfobject" failure, no matter how historically driven, has eroded my self-confidence, already weakened by guilt about my erotic counter-transference. There is a combination here of her projections (or expectations based on experience, really) and my tendency to a sense of guilty inadequacy. Somewhat akin to the idea of the projection "hook," this can also be further described this way: the analyst introjectively identifies along the lines of his own complexes.

9.

Transference	Countertransference
F described feelings of admiration, trust, and attraction for a man in a position of authority at work.	I knew of this man, who presented himself as very self-assured. I didn't like him (especially now).
She was excited when he admitted having (undefined) feelings for her – to her this meant he was "vulnerable" and she could have some "power" over him.	Though I thought this image/experience of him might be a transference displacement (from me), I still felt inadequate compared to him and relatively "powerless."
She fantasized that I would be "jealous" about this and hence also vulnerable to her.	Was I jealous, as she suggested? And was she some kind of mindreader?
Next F sheepishly told me she had sexual fantasies of being with two men at the same time. She had literally enacted this in the past with her husband's participation and apparent encouragement.	Pinned down by her intuition and turned on by her fantasies, I did feel vulnerable to her. I felt relieved that her attentions were directed elsewhere – it would give me time to pull myself together.

Discussion

The patient's unconscious will not only induce or infect the analyst's, it will then see right through it. This is the source of the attribution sometimes made to difficult patients: they have an uncanny and embarrassing knack for finding the analyst's weaknesses. I am here struggling without much success to conceal this and be comfortable with the countertransference position I find myself in. At times this is a question of endurance. As Jung says, "Difficult cases are a veritable ordeal" (Jung, 1951a, p. 116). Her two-man fantasy, here in its most recent edition, is being enacted with the supervisor and me. In a general way this was not unlike my own two-woman issue. The countertransference, again, is an amalgam of her fast-moving, potent projective identifications and my pre-existing, parallel tendencies. The therapist's readiness to feel a certain way can be worked over by the patient, seemingly mercilessly.

10.

Transference	Countertransference
After canceling a session, F said, "I missed you . . . I couldn't enjoy the flowers without you . . . I never want to go without two sessions [per week] with you again."	*This sounded pretty romantic to me. Her dependency seemed positive but I feared I could not meet it properly, due to my own "romantic" fantasies. I worried that her need to feel "special" should not be met by my (incestuous? re-traumatizing?) desires.*

Discussion

These are continued efforts to contain and re-route the countertransference to fit the patient's perceived need. But the analyst's feelings cannot be artificially altered or role-played. Changes have to be authentic – and the patient has to wait. Actually my attempt to provide nurturing rather than sexualized eros may reflect her own confusion of the two (due to an actual or emotional incest situation or, along the same lines, her father's difficulty in separating the two). If so, I am now carrying this "boundary" conflict from her psyche and history. By holding and struggling directly (personally, as it were) with the patient's conflict, the therapist may also be embodying a growth tendency in the patient that is trying or starting to form. Thus the analyst's "infected" state might also be called a "prospective countertransference." One hopes that the appropriate, needed response is in the making.

11.

Transference	Countertransference
Referring to someone she knew, F said, "I don't think I can hold someone — how much I need that from you! . . . If father could only have admitted his weakness. I see him as being totally false . . . . I don't trust anything."	*I struggled internally with the questions: can I hold her properly, should I admit my "weakness," am I "totally false" and hiding behind a professional persona?*
She went on, "The blank screen can't be genuine . . . . If I had power over you, I could trust you more."	*I felt almost overwhelming pressure here to confess my attraction, inadequacy and her power but . . .*
Returning to the "other man" theme, F noted it was tough to separate "friendship from the physical . . . . He [the man] gets involved."	*. . . who was she talking about? Me, father, friends? And would such a self-disclosure be the trust-engendering "holding" she requested or . . .*
She added, "Why would he want to be friends if it wasn't sexual?"	*. . . the opposite? Namely, another reminder that her only value was sexual.*

Discussion

The therapist is now in a cloudy state of near-total introjective identification, trying to find some footing. The line between "neurotic" and "complementary" countertransference is blurred. But the blur between "sex/friendship" may in itself be "syntonic" with F's similar confusion. Disclosing countertransference reactions to a patient is a dicey issue, requiring intuition, subtleties of feeling and, in my opinion, reserve[2]. Particularly when the therapist feels muddled, containment would seem to be the rule, as the possibility of acting out is strong then. Early in the analysis this might especially be the case.

12.

Transference	Countertransference
[As this session continued, I noted to F that there did seem to be "some sexual attraction in the field between us."]	*Unwilling to admit "weakness" as my own, exclusively, I do at least acknowledge the sexual dimension she's been alluding to.*
[I suggested this field paralleled that between her and her father, and that the feelings were mutual between them.]	*My countertransference-based, transference interpretation felt accurate but possibly self-defensive under these circumstances.*
F said, "I don't want it from him. I don't want to want it. I don't think I should have to . . . I don't want to love him again. [Why?] I just want to shut the door."	*I had some feeling I was pushing her to admit that she did love and have sexual feelings for her father.*

Discussion

There is an attempt here to make some sense of the complex transference/countertransference interplay. It is again unclear if, in wanting F to "accept" my interpretation, I am: 1) acting out the father's side of an incestuous relationship, or 2) trying to get her to "admit" having feelings for me (in the guise of father), or 3) trying to get her to admit what I wouldn't (attraction to her). A countertransference-based interpretation, such as this was, needs fairly close monitoring as to its deflecting, defusing value. The interpretation may be true, or even desirable to relieve a murky situation, but it may simultaneously be defensive or disengaging. Plaut's ideas about "incarnating" the archetype and Schwartz-Salant's on "sacrificing" interpretations may be relevant here. On the other hand the analyst's relative "safety" (and the patient's) can be relevant too (Plaut, 1956, p. 157).

13. Countertransference fantasies

F's father then happened to be in town and she was late for the session. As I waited, I speculated in writing:

51

More confusion about times:

– retaliation for sexual-father-approval linkage?

– to see if I'm keyed up and reacting, or jealous?

– Or because I didn't act more human or less "blank screen?"

Wants firm bounds against sexual exploitation she also sends out or has been recipient of.

Fantasy: something happened with father. Father said she couldn't go/come.

[20 minutes late] Fantasy: quitting? Fantasy: battle over missed session? (I'll note and maybe not charge, probably will charge if she was not just unclear.) Unclear due to my not setting firm bounds (2X/week) she needs?

To see if I'll call her? I imagine she'll be huffy that I didn't, though she missed the session."

Session

F arrived 25 minutes late, saying her lateness felt "dissociated." She spoke of retaliating against her father and husband for talking just to each other, and not to her. She thought her lateness might be a response to my linking sexual issues and father in the last session. She wanted to see if I would go overtime, to see if I was thinking about her. F said: *"I want you to fall in love with me, but need you not to."*

Discussion

Analytic sessions begin psychologically at the appointed hour, and a patient's lateness may be fruitfully used by attending to the countertransference that is inevitably generated. The therapist's hypotheses, self-states and fantasies fill the vacuum of the patient's absence, forming an image, accurate or inaccurate, of what is in the patient's mind.

Here my fantasies mostly correspond to the feeling states and needs she subsequently reveals. A syntonic countertransference emerges from a boundaryless place, which paradoxically results in a clear, bordered one. Even as I continued to ponder boundary issues before her arrival, she defined in a succinct and profound way the *exact* (and paradoxical) type of boundary she needed: "I want you to fall in love with me, but need you not to." This was the very countertransference I had been struggling with.

14. Patient's dream

I am smoking pot with S [her male friend/higher-up at work] and I touch him. I'm hanging around, waiting for him.

(Associations: "I feel touched to the core by his directness".)

Transference	Countertransference
F said, "I feel like a spider, trying to lure you in with talk about sex." She first felt shame, but later added she didn't feel "accused" by me (i.e. guilty).	I didn't really think of F as a spider, but she did continue to have a certain bewitching effect on me.
She said she still wanted to "deny" positive feelings or needs for her father.	I asked myself, "What about the 'missing Mother?' – little said about her."
F said Mother was institutionalized, "possibly schizophrenic," when F was young.	As if answering my silent question.

Countertransference notes (post-session)

"Aware of feeling less tension in session. Partly due to my exhaustion? But perhaps more due to less sexual tension making things less exciting. The sexual issue, promise was gone. Indeed I did feel a little jealous that she was feeling this authority and fertilization ['touched to core' in the dream] with S, not me.

Here I am, midlife, balding, tired, wife pregnant, cancer under my arm yielding deep intimations of mortality (as well as fathers' deaths)[3]. And I am getting a charge out of this attractive, fairly swinging, sometimes available 'Jungian' female.

Though I told her it was 'analysis only' here, her 'I want you to love me but need you not to' has been acting on me directly. I was indeed disappointed that, in my fantasy at least, this woman was not directing her charms toward me. I felt the loss."

Discussion

I *had been* lured in. She felt guilty about it, though she had astutely recognized its necessity (i.e. "want you to fall in love with me . . ."). I am finally able to admit it "out loud" to myself here. Admission of the so-called "neurotic" countertransference allows its amplification-clarification: my mid-life issues are then seen to fit the patient's "love me – but don't" transference program to a T. Furthermore, I can then "participate" in that emotionally corrective program more readily. With this shift too comes the idea of the mother in her associations and mine. This may have something to do with the downturn in the sexual dynamic – from father to mother.

15.

Transference	Countertransference
F discussed her own psychiatric hospitalization as a teenager.	I saw F as a sexually available, wild teenager, like girls I'd known in the adolescent unit of a psychiatric hospital where I once worked.
Her father, court-appointed guardian and stepfather had accused her of promiscuity as a teen, she said.	I thought of Salem "witch trials" and imagined these men were projecting their own desires into her.

Discussion

While it is one thing to hear about, it is another thing for the therapist to "see" the patient in time. Via my own images I could envision F and what her life then might have been like. Perhaps this empathic effort had a different feeling tone than that of paternal figures at the time. On her part F may have sensed that I too might desire, project and accuse in similar fashion.

Part of the difficulty of the countertransference is that the therapist may carry many or all of the patient's unconscious states at the same time. Thus I could identify with her ego position against the hypocritical "fathers," while I was also potentially one of "them" (bewitched by this woman, or my anima).

16.

Transference	Countertransference
F described her positive feelings about her friend S and worries that "his wife" might feel threatened.	I wondered in a Langsian way if these were references to her situation with me as well.
"It is appealing to me to balance or complement what another person doesn't have. To fill that, in them . . . the unconscious, intuitive, irrational."	She certainly seemed to be an "anima" woman to everybody, including me.

Discussion

I was having distinct ideas of reference here. Her fantasy and sometime experience of herself as a hetaera type certainly corresponded to aspects of my countertransference and "other woman" fantasies. From this perspective she is wondering if my marriage can tolerate this. It is not accurate to say, however, that these were strictly "analytic interaction" images – they were simultaneously factual, historical-Oedipal, historical with husband, interactive, and so on. All could be true. As with the understanding of any other unconscious product, countertransference is subject to a pluralistic or "simultaneous" interpretation; that is, there are multiple meanings possible. The question that arises is where to put the leverage.

17.

Transference	Countertransference
[F's husband called to say she would be late for the session. I said, formally, "Thank you for calling."]	I felt uneasy talking to him. A little afraid or guilty?

Discussion

The intimate and eroticized transference/countertransference made me uncomfortable: the incestuous or secret "affair" might be seen by the father-rival-husband-superego. Also the therapist knows the spouse's "secrets" as revealed by the patient. Numerous taboos and trusts are broken in analysis. The countertransference "shadow" of an analyst is informed not just by neurotic, Oedipal, voyeuristic, power-seeking or narcissistic motives; "original sin" and incestuous guilt are involved.

18. Patient's dreams

1. *My husband makes sexual overtures to me and I'm aroused. But I can't because my father is in the next room.*

2. *I'm with you at a round table on a mountain top near a little house at night. People are in the valley below. We may be talking about the previous dream, or my [eldest] brother. You suggest to me that I should sing. My response is, "I guess that would turn down the heat."*

Transference	Countertransference
About me in the dream F felt it was "wonderful that you're there . . . inside me . . . in that important part."	*I in part heard these initial statements ("inside me") as having a lot of confusing sexual innuendo.*
However, she experienced my dream suggestion [to sing] as "turning down the intensity . . . You are rejecting me, like father . . . I feel hurt."	*Aware of the mutual "heat," I had been trying to tone things down. I felt badly that I couldn't, in her eyes, manage the erotic intensity.*
F felt that heat related to "animals in heat . . . hard to say it – sex."	*I felt guilty for feeling "erotic" and now guilty for deflecting it.*

Discussion

Sometimes it's hard to be an analyst. The first dream shed light on the father complex interfering with F's sex life and eros. It perhaps had some bearing on my earlier countertransference discomfort with F's husband as well (see section 17, p. 55), with me as the interfering father. I did not want to embody or perpetuate the apparently incestuous father relationship, but feared I was, through my induced or predisposed countertransference.

56

Yet it was plain from the second dream and the in-session innuendo that diversions from the heated transference/counter-transference *eros* were looked on critically by the dream ego (*I* had thought my asking her to "sing" was not so bad, given her narcissistic issues). To be in a client's dream poses again the subjective/objective dilemma in understanding: is it me or is it the "therapist" imago – or is it both? Or is it perhaps, from a slightly different perspective, a necessary "grounding" of the transference for the analyst to be deeply caught up in the counter-transference?

19.

Transference	*Countertransference*
F said she had called my answering tape to "hear" my voice after a big fight with her husband. At the end of the session, she suddenly asked if she could call me at home, if necessary.	*I felt hamstrung, again. I didn't want to appear cold and I knew her dependency needs were emerging, but this was not quite an emergency and it didn't feel right to meet this request.*
[I said, "My number is there on the tape. . . . People have been known to call me."]	*My remarks felt "undecided" to me (as they in fact were) and sort of asinine.*

Discussion

This was somewhat like previous "frame" pressures – reduced fees, insurance, etc. – in which she pushed, then I felt pulled because of the strong countertransference, and finally I set a limit. Only this time I split, and confusingly suggested one thing while feeling but not quite admitting another. This was the first in a series of sessions in which I seemed to fail F empathically.

Working from countertransference or any other position requires making many delicate "feeling" decisions in the context of the patient's transference states. Mistakes are inevitable, and maybe even necessary. The failure here was less in the choice per se than in its ambiguity and inauthenticity.

20.

Transference	Countertransference
At the end of one of several sessions in which she had wept occasionally, described lost-child imagery and noted how "inept" her father was emotionally, F asked if I had anything to say about what she'd just said.	*I felt a certain demand from her to comment but was unable to "tie the threads" together.*
	I was aware of time running out in the hour and recalled times when my own analyst never said a word.
[I said, "I don't think so," but did remind her of an upcoming time change.]	*I thought she might be mad and that I might have seemed abrupt, or withholding.*

Discussion

I seemed to be demonstrating and probably embodying the same ineptitude her father reportedly had in earlier times of abandonment. I had felt worthless when my analyst said nothing. Whether or not there were residual angers or identifications from my own analysis or whether this was a complementary "negative father" (or mother) countertransference, it would still be experienced as an empathic failure here and now. Mistakes come from the analyst and cannot be rationalized away as patient "induction." However, they may not be mistakes of blind "countertransference." Rather, they may be "speed" problems; that is, mistakes where the therapist is not quite up to speed in his processing. For example, here the empathic countertransference fantasies are moving in the right direction, toward a syntonic understanding (how I once felt, how she might feel), but I don't quite make it.

21.

Transference	Countertransference
Angry and wounded, F said in the next session, "I see you fused with my father."	*I knew I had hurt F, however inadvertently, with my holding or empathic failure.*

Like him, I gave her only "structure" but not support, and like her father and husband I was essentially "powerless, helpless and weak."

As she dressed me down, I was reminded of a mentor's remark about how vital it was to be able to really get mad at his analyst.

She felt "lost in the crowd" of my other patients. She cried copiously and noted her "terror that if I don't get attention, I won't survive."

While she wept, I felt the impulse to reach out and touch her on the shoulder in a kindly way. I decided it would be inappropriate to do so.

Patient's dream

Her husband's good friend had full breasts.

[Associations: this friend was one of the "other men" she was attracted to. She recalled the dream with disappointment after expressing her doubts about me and other men: "Is this how men are? Fuck men. There's this hole in men."]

Discussion

My recent mistake(s) fortunately resulted in therapeutic movement, thanks to her steadfastness (and perhaps her compensatory dream). She was trying to move into a position of trust with me and I seemed to keep flunking it. I was unclear why I kept missing her needs of the moment. I appeared to "be," or be re-traumatizing her like, her presumably incompetent, form-without-substance father. As in the dream, the idea of nurturance was somehow tied up with the male, and with me in the transference (and with sexuality). My impulse to reach out gently, though not acted upon, indicated I had temporarily at least got to the more maternal, less breast-less and less rigidly paternal place she needed. It also corresponded to various dreams and in-session feelings where F had felt "touched" (by me or Mr. S, her supervisor). Thus what may be seen here is a movement from an empathic failure to what might be called a compensatory or corrective countertransference. If the therapist is really embodying certain aspects of the client's psyche, then such shifts in the therapist may have modifying effect on the constellated complex(es).

22.

Transference	Countertransference
F described her father being a member of a well-known public figure's entourage.	*Though she'd once told me this, I now "realized" I had indeed heard of her father.*
She then added, "You may have read some of his [her father's] books."	*I hadn't, but I suddenly recalled there was one on the shelves when I was growing up.*
She then looked around my office to see, she said, if there were any of them there.	*I was struck by the parallel history and these space/time shifts between us.*

Discussion

This interesting coincidence caused a dynamic shift in my image of F. First, I "saw" her background as more sophisticated than her anti-intellectual persona let on. Second, I began to see it, and her family, as very like my own. Before, I had tended to see much of her experience as somewhat alien. Now, as I reflected further on it, I could see strong similarities not only in terms of cultural milieu but quite specifically in terms of certain political, philosophical and even personal factors. There was some parallel history. Somehow this hadn't dawned on me consciously until this rapid oscillation of in-session associations between her and me took place. Though there were differences in degree perhaps, the alienated "inner patient" in me could now hook up with this actual patient much more deeply. Matching histories or backgrounds are not necessary for this to happen, but they can help deepen the identification when they occur.

23.

Transference	Countertransference
In the next session F mentioned "potholes," a dead rabbit in the road and construction workers hooting at her on the way to session.	*I played internally with the idea of her analytic "path" and imagined this college friend of mine who acted like these workers.*

She looked at my license on the wall and asked about my background.	*Given her recent criticisms, I heard her credentials check as critical of me.*
After expressing her desire for "an emotionally available, regular, nurturing figure," F added that she wanted to be an analyst, too.	*"Probably be a better one than I am," I thought, feeling depressed about my ability to give her a motherly* agape *rather than a lover's* eros.

Discussion

The basic trust issue continues. In the wake of recent empathic failures and my desire (perhaps imaged, respectively, by the rocky road with dead rabbits and my whistling construction-worker inclinations), I sincerely doubted my ability to be emotionally trustworthy. However, even this seemingly private woundedness could have been relevant to F's hurt feelings or her own parents' similar doubts. In fact what later became clear was F's powerful guilt and despair about her failure to "cure" her own mother. Countertransference states do not seem to be discrete – they are fluid, and simultaneously operating at different levels. Thus, here, there is something like a "triple" countertransference: my neurotic-depressive one, a complementary one (me as failing parent), and a syntonic one (like her, I feel inadequate to cure the person who needs it).

At the time, though, what I experienced was the truth of her accusations (section 21, pp. 58–59) about my typically male incompetence, much as I heard her credentials check as criticism rather than a desire to be "just like me" – an analyst. It may be important for the therapist to experience such depressive states as really "his own" – to be truly "infected," or truly *in* his own inner "patient" – in order to ground authentically the healing process.

24. Patient's dream

There's a Tarzan-like, beast-man in my mother's rose garden. I say, "He's learned to speak surprisingly well."

I call you on the phone, then wonder, "Why are you calling him?" You react like you've been at a wedding and are drunk, though you're not. You tell me about the wedding as a way of telling me you can't see me. You have to have a tooth extracted by Dr. X.

Now we're in the living room with your wife. You still are really helpless. Me and your wife are figuring out how to pull it together. You're sort of out of control but it feels good that the women are pulling it out. I feel close with your wife.

Countertransference

Transference dreams may first of all be checked for countertransferential truth. I wondered how I might be linked to this primitive Tarzan figure, but decided it connected with her mother. However, I was dismayed by the objective viewpoint that I was "out of control" like this, and F and my anima-wife were trying to help me out. The image certainly corresponded with some of my guilty feelings about not being "good enough" as analyst or even as a person. I felt embarrassed too, within this identification with her dream-healer, that my patient was caring for me, not vice versa, and sardonically noted to myself, "She is working with my anima, in solidarity, even though I don't know what the hell I'm doing."

Discussion

As indicated by my embarrassed, guilty identification, it seemed we were at the point where the transference had really "taken." I was hooked by, and my own feelings had provided the hooks for, her projection *and* what it was aiming at – namely, the rehabilitation of the drunken, out of control or helpless nurturer/mother/father/therapist. I wasn't sure which, though I thought the mother was herein more implicated due to her alcoholic history. If F's dream of my "wife" did refer to my anima, then it was promising that F was positively linked with my unconscious while my conscious position was indeed that of feeling weak or powerless (to use her terms). Such "countertransference defeats," difficult as they may be for the therapist's ego (or his grandiosity), may often be necessary.

25.

Transference	Countertransference
F said she liked the above dream picture of me, not in my rigid, father-like "work" persona but my "real self."	*I didn't like it one bit. I felt very uneasy, and a bit wounded that she saw me as "unreal."*

Her friend, S, was changing jobs and "desperately desired" F to join him. F "loved being so wanted."

I felt her right inside me, enticing and working on me to open up, desire and "want" her like S had.

She spoke to me of the "firm strength not to need the boundaries . . . not denying yourself your need to be taken care of."

"Who is analyzing whom?" I thought. I fantasized she wanted me to "go first," to let go a little so she could.

[I suggested her desire for me to open up was about her anxiety and need to open up her own, vulnerable self.]

I didn't like any of this much, and couldn't accept her apparent offer to assuage my unmet dependency needs.

Discussion

A great, seductive push from her to let my hair down: a difficult task for me to incarnate that but also meet the other need (for me "not to be" seduced or seduce her). So I put the ball back in her court. I felt no real danger of actually acting out, but was resistant to admitting and possibly burdening her with my fantasies. The wanting she wanted – which I thought was early, "child"-like and narcissistic (in a positive sense) – was not the wanting I generally felt, which was more "adult" (hence incestuous in the context of her "child" need). If I "let go," what she would get would be an untrustworthy and incestuous father, again, or the "out of control" mother. As I wanted above all to be a good parent-analyst to her, I had to contain myself despite her invitation to reverse roles. In the absence of a viable mother, F may have turned to father. This may have accounted for the incestuous-Oedipal feel of our analytic relationship and for the clouded mix of mother (drunk, needing care) and father (too rigid) in the dream and in session.

26.

Transference

After I interpreted in a session F's need to feel "completely important," she said she couldn't with me "because you have other clients."

Countertransference

She did feel to me like my "most important" patient, or at least the one I most looked forward to seeing, usually.

Leaving, F said she wanted to talk more about her husband because "he is the most important man in my life."	*"I'm not!" I wrote. "Feeling with her of exclusivity, her and me, = very pleasant." Now I felt disappointment.*

Discussion

The therapist and patient trade narcissistic needs back and forth, retaliating as they go, as if in a jealous lovers' or siblings' quarrel. The deeper fusion of recent weeks is thus continuing, with elements of a syntonic countertransference.

27. Countertransference fantasies and dream

I awakened at 3 a.m. on a hot summer night and began thinking about F. I then fell into the following dream:

F appears not as a sultry adult but as an 8–9-year-old pre-teen girl. She gets hit by a flying object behind the eye. Though she's unhurt, I worry that she might be embarrassed.

My own son then awoke with a nightmare and I rushed in to comfort him. I noticed the paternal feeling I was having toward both him and F (in the dream of her) and, following this, began to reflect on my own wounds, narcissistic and otherwise, in the aftermath of my own parents' divorce when I was 8–9. I thought, interpreting objectively, that the blow to her head might be my fantasizing about her.

Discussion

This synchronicity of wounds in three heads (F's in my dream, mine and my son's) permits a further differentiation of the sexual from the parental and a still deeper understanding of the complex identification with F. She was even more "part of the family" now. Having incorporated her through the father-book-my house-my office sequence (section 22, p. 60), she is now visioned in my present family, too, and linked more directly with my own child and "wounded child." This marks a further movement toward providing in the countertransference more of what F "needed" and more of what I too felt she needed (however reluctant I was to give her up as an object of desire). The therapist's unconscious, if struggled with, will slowly begin to move in directions the patient requires. Also, just as the therapist introjects the patient into his family, so the patient's transference will contain projections that are played out in fantasies about the therapist's family, as noted before (see pp. 55, 60, 61–62).

28.

Transference	*Countertransference*
F took the job in the same place as Mr. S. She was smiling and sheepish with me.	I fantasized she'd leave her work with me.
She fantasized that I'd be jealous, that this was like going off with a boyfriend and leaving a jealous father.	I wrote of S post-session: "This dynamic dude, older, more confident. . . . I do feel some competitive loss, her preferring S."
She'd "do anything to stay in therapy," and wondered if once a week would be OK.	Though she reassured me, I felt the loss.
[At the end, I congratulated her on her new job].	This felt hollow. I later wrote, "I need to be therapist, not friend, to her."

Discussion

I am fully engaged with her feelings/projections here, and walking the line between being possessed by them and seeing how I was "incarnating" the abandoned, jealous father-boyfriend. Among the more painful aspects of working via countertransference is "joining" up with triangles like these; letting countertransference *feelings* and not just images "lead the way" can be like leading with your chin, as the boxers say.

29.

Transference	*Countertransference*
Unable to get a sitter, F (unannounced) brought her child into a session.	A test, a concretization? I felt surprised and a little irritated.

Invited to explore this, F saw me as "rigid and intellectual."	*I pondered the "rejecting father" in me. I felt pressure to be nice to her kid.*
She added, "Your neutrality bugs me. . . . There has to be love, too, and humanness in this process . . . . Accessibility has always been a problem here, like your fees."	*Am I such a feeling-less creep? She's trying to force something on me, while also saying, "Don't let me" (as in "love me, but don't")?*
F fantasized about her little girl "doing anything in here." [I said she could do anything, short of hurting herself. I gave her a toy rhino and helped her up one time.]	*I rather enjoyed the feeling of her, me and her daughter – the three of us. After the session I noted my fantasies to myself, "I want to be Number 1, not S or her husband."*
She was, however, pleased by my "gentleness" with her girl.	*I had felt pressure to be a "good" father, and had passed.*

Discussion

There is more of the complex "family" byplay here, with me being "familiar," it seemed, across two generations. First, there was the sense that I was her father in this psychodrama and she was observing how I might "be" with her child-self. Second, I was in the place, and enjoying it, of her husband, the "current" family. This was our exclusive triad and my triangular victory. The further deepening into family, on two levels, is also an extension of movements cited above (sections 22, 24, 27). The "analytic marriage," like an actual marriage, consists of the intertwining of not just two persons, but of their "families" (the family history and atmosphere of each, and the family of shared introjects). Searles (1977, p. 470) amusingly speaks of experiencing certain patients as "a tribe" (of introjects). In this kind of analytic engagement two tribes come together.

30. Patient's dream (during vacation break)

My car's been stolen. I drive a similar car, realizing the cops will think I've stolen it. I see a dual-image:

1) My mother driving my car into my father's driveway. 2) My mother being carried into an ICU on a stretcher.

I see my mother's face all anguished and contorted, and I am wailing in horror. I'm aware I may be disturbing people in this hospital, where babies are also being born. When I look again, she has become a blob of bloody tissue, like an aborted fetus. How can this ever be whole again, be resurrected?

I hear her say "Mama." At that moment it dawns on me that I am not her mother. That's someone else. I can't be; that's someone else's place.

An older woman approaches me and says, "What a shame for this to happen so late in life." I answer curtly, "It's happened before," referring to her earlier suicide attempt.

I realize in the dream I never felt or expressed any of this before, all the horror, wailing, disgust and terror.

[Background associations: "When I was 13, mother attempted suicide at my father's house when my father was away with his lover." When F saw her mother in coma, F had felt she "never could go home again, mother had died, and I had abandoned her."]

F dreamed this obviously "big dream" after the last session before a long vacation break. During the break she wrote me three, unsent, diary-like letters (in one of which this dream was included). She read me the letters and dream in the session after her return, which follows:

Transference	*Countertransference*
[F decried her "dead" father in her letter:]	
"My life is shot through with all my hatred of him, all the twisted eroticism and deprivation. The decision he made long ago to kill his inner self and mutilate the souls of those around him."	*This was what she projected into and feared in me. It seemed so extreme, I could see that it was not me, at least not to this degree.*
About this, F wrote, "I felt the grief wash through me, and the only face I could see was yours and the only hope to break through it."	*This felt like a love letter. I was pleased to be her hope, unlike her father.*

F described her mother's dream-face: "A face, but nothing else. No face. A bloody glob like an aborted fetus."	*I felt tears begin to well up. I recalled the amazement I felt when an analyst actually cried at something I said.*
She then broke down in tears.	*I was pleased my empathy was tuned in, even a touch ahead.*

Discussion

In the syntonic countertransference there is both separation here from the projective/introjective identification and a moving emotional connection in depth. The possibility of my face as an empathic rather than a distorted mirror is explored, all this being the opposite of the dream-mother's aborted and father's allegedly mutilated face. Recent efforts within me perhaps permit or at least synchronize with F's being able to arrive in the dream at the healing idea that she need not feel responsible for mother's desperate needs.

32. Patient's dream

I'm in your office, which is in the French Quarter of New Orleans. You're in jeans, more yourself. You're talking to your ex-wife on the phone about your daughter. You tell me about your next wife – she's won awards for "moral purity." Then you're talking to your present girl friend, with whom you are freer, more relaxed.

We're both looking out the window at fire engines. People are looking up and I don't see the fire. I look closely in their eyes and can only see the reflection of the fire there. They're looking up at our window.

The fire is inside me and I feel it burning. All this feeling and desire and passion that's been trapped in there.

I'm thinking theoretically about a man trapped in the building. How will he know he needs help? How can he be saved if he doesn't know there's a problem?

I'm outside now trying to find your apartment building. A woman inside says it's cool to live here, inviting me in.

Transference	Countertransference
When telling me this dream, F said she copied it in "blue, the color of your eyes."	*I liked this but laughed a bit inside: my eyes are green [and love is blind].*
[My assorted ex- and "morally pure" wives and the new, "freer" girlfriend]	*Her? Her wish? Is she again seeing through me, to my evolving inner/feeling states?*
[The "fires" inside her, being in my office, burning and "trapped" desires]	*I felt a rise in my penis and was glad I had a note pad in my lap to cover in case.*
[The fire engines]	*I was glad they were around.*
[Swinging New Orleans. Her association: "A Streetcar Named Desire"]	*I thought how it was dark, late and she was my last patient. A steamy situation.*
[The "trapped" man who needs "help"]	*I wondered if this referred to me.*

As the session continued under this (for me) intense pressure, I decided to just hold on, frankly unable to analyze anything at the moment. I reminded her of her "wise" words about wanting me to fall in love with her, though needing me not to. I wrote immediately after the hour that all I could do was "contain, maintain and *appear* neutral." I also noted how I had been tempted in this sultry atmosphere to appear clever, or impressively wise.

Discussion

Under fire of an erotic transference/countertransference the therapist sometimes can only sit on it until he is able to manage it in some way. As Jung says,

> the philosophers suffer very much from the intense heat during their confinement. . . . The modern equivalent of this stage is the unconscious realization of sexual fantasies which color the transference accordingly.
>
> Jung, 1946, pp. 245–246

Further clarification started the next night.

33. *Countertransference reflections* (next night)

In session: difficult to maintain analytic stance against focussed, very positive transference (erotic). Pressure to share, not analyze this experience with her.

I was also aware not of coldness but of a professional, even, neutral quality to my writing down of her dream – not getting excited.

Fantasy: some question in my mind of my ability to work with her under this internal/external pressure. Will [my supervisor] kick me out of analysis with her?!

(3 a.m.) She = like pornography, though not dirty/sexual, more eros/flame style. She = a siren, seducing me, amongst the others in succession? Fantasy: me, like others, shot down → resentment and anger [several old girlfriends came to mind] – i.e. neg. anima.

She comes on with: looks (demure, looking away), tight clothes, sexual stories (past and present), confessions (like these dreams, letters), neg. relationship with husband, "lost waif" history.

Therefore, my position: to hold on, not reject, not be submerged in non-analytic transference resistance.

It's awfully nice to be "the man of her dreams" but I notice also a kind of empty quality. Turned on, but where's the beef of it? I don't know her, really, nor do I really want to (in that erotic sense). There's some-thing constellated and exciting, but there's a flatness in it. There's not really a question of acting out. I couldn't imagine it really happening. It hits me in that anima spot – the dreams of the other woman.

Fantasy: this is a test, and she's got all the burners going. Flattering me, this beautiful woman, in love with me. A test: to not shut her out, defensively, and to not fall into it, non-analytically.

Fantasy (3 a.m.): hers = like a love letter, waiting to be read. Fantasy (now): a kind of torture for me. "Longing" constellated but denied. Fantasy (post-session): talk to [supervisor] soon!

Discussion

When the countertransference gets too "hot," the therapist has to shut down. Introspection becomes the technical measure to get oneself started again. There was a sense in which I was with her

– sharing the exciting desires – but also one in which I was behind her: I felt she needed me to be able to handle this high "intensity" more easily. But I was still struggling with the complicated "induction" she had earlier outlined of both falling and not falling in love with her. My above reflections show my circumambulation of this – sometimes guilty, sometimes accusatory, hopeless, tortured and so on. The words of the psychoanalyst Lucia Tower (1956, p. 232) on the virtual necessity of "countertransference neurosis" were relevant if not totally reassuring, as were those of Harold Searles:

> I have found, time after time, that in the course of work with every one of my patients who has progressed to, or very near towards, a thoroughgoing analytic cure, I have experienced romantic and erotic desires to marry, and fantasies of being married to, the patient.
>
> (Searles, 1959, p. 284)

34. Patient's dream

My husband's friend X – the feeling of him recognizing me, seeing me. He wanted to marry me.

[Associations: "I'm jealous of his relationship with my husband. I wish he'd be devoted to me." (X was the same friend who appeared earlier "with full breasts" – see section 21, pp. 58–59)].

Countertransference fantasies (shortly after this dream)

Fantasy: S [her work friend] has the big penis and I feel inadequate. This → a push to show her how smart I am and her to approve of it: "you're good."

My fantasy: not acting out, but I'm more subtly in this game of attraction and "Will she like me?" – i.e. early seduction. [I have some] reluctance to give up that way of being, though.

And here she is with the love letters, "Fire" in the heart, transference positive, and the triangle challenge (to win her).

Fantasy: I and my wife = her friends. I want to be "special" to her. (She wants that from me, for the right reasons).

What man wouldn't fall for this sexy, vulnerable woman? And she says she wants to be someone's anima-inspiratrice. A woman-geisha, by your side.

71

Maybe S = not superior, but in the trap. Showing off for her! (this = first fantasy where S is not superior, is like me).

Discussion

As I backed off to work through my side of the erotic fantasy, which had competitive and narcissistic dimensions, she dreams of a man (me?, conceivably) who wants to "marry" her. Meanwhile, I find in me the same fantasy she often had of being "special." We both wanted to be approved by and "devoted to" one another, it seemed. But until I could get a steadier hold on things on my end, I felt I could not comfortably let her work out her feelings on me – for fear I would infect her with mine. Our complexes were mixing, in order to re-form, but the initial responsibility to work out the mix lay with me, the therapist.

35. Countertransference reflections

The countertransference has kept me from seeing it [certain dream interpretations]. [The idea arises of] free-flowing into understanding of her being more important than a relationship with her played out in session.

This feels like giving her up.

→ *parallels with her father, who gave her up too quickly, possibly due to inappropriate eroticism?*

→ *fantasies about my daughter & giving up and erotic feelings toward.*

(one week later) Seeing her as a child who doesn't know what she is doing.

– from a woman to a child in my eyes.

Discussion

As can be seen, a fair amount of countertransference work happens not during but in between sessions. Here, I continue to fantasize about F and find her again linking in my mind with my "family," though this time with my then two-month-old daughter. These musings are amplifications of the feeling spaces between the patient and therapist. The subject appears to be father–daughter incest. These are the first indications of an authentic movement, however unfinished and glacial, in my various feeling states.

36. Countertransference (before session)

One week later, I received a letter from a former analyst of mine. He told me he was dating a friend of mine who had been a former patient of his. I was disturbed and angry about this, particularly as I was trying to sort out the emotional dilemmas of my often triangulated countertransference to F.

I noticed as I went into session that I was wearing casual clothes like my former analyst's and enjoyed this identification with him – being "like" him. I knew too that F preferred this kind of style (see section 25, pp. 62–63). I had also become aware that I would sometimes think of F as I chose my clothes on days she had a session. For instance, I would think of not wearing a tie so she wouldn't accuse me of being "uptight" or a "square." At any rate she was the woman I found myself wanting to dress for, the woman whose opinion was important.

Patient's dream (in session)

I'm in the town I grew up in. I realize my life is falling apart. I drive about, having missed a session with you. I feel the pain, like in August [vacation], like the forlorn feeling I grew up with magnified 100 times.

I go to your office. Your wife is there. (Though late) I have no doubt you'll see me. We look for a place to meet privately.

Your arm is around my shoulder some of the time, and it surprises me it feels good and sort of protective. I wonder, "Is it OK? Why is he doing it?" You touch me with your hand: maybe that's what I need to heal it, feeling "loved."

Now we're at a dimly lit bar and climb to a loft. We have a romantic-sexual contact – I don't remember which? Really spiritual, not carnal. I'm on top of you and keep trying to prop up your head with a pillow. There's a hole in the floor under your head. A sense of adventure.

Then there's a change – your hair is thinner, whiter, older. I don't recognize you and desire cools. I'm more aware of you as a physical being? Is this really what I want?

Transference	Countertransference
F associated to some secret sexual meetings in high school with a boy up in his room. He had a girlfriend.	I wondered about her and me, "up here" in my dimly lit office, me with a "wife" (just as he had a "girlfriend"?).

F spoke of "propping up" her parents and of incest victims "reassuring" their parents.	I felt guilty that, again, she might be helping me more than I her . . .
The older man resembled a suite mate of mine: "a fraud, it was just sexual."	. . . and that I was just a dirty young/old man, and she could see it.
F felt no boundaries between sex and other feelings. All touch was sexual.	[I noted to her the sexual vibes in our meetings but stressed the boundaries here.]
All this was sort of an "amorphous mass" of feelings.	I was reminded of the dream of mother's "aborted" face.

Discussion

Again in my introjective identification, combined with my own erotic countertransference, I emotionally take on in session the role of the incest propagator. Though this dream had some of the potential "fire" of the earlier "New Orleans" dream (section 32, pp. 68–69), I am now able to draw the appropriate line – in the earlier session I just couldn't speak. This is a result of: 1) my recent countertransference workings through, 2) the dream itself with its disillusioning conclusion, and 3) arriving at my own disillusioning but strongly felt criticism of my former analyst's questionable (from what I knew of it), "incestuous" behavior.

There seemed to be important parallel processes in F's and my mutual disappointments, but perhaps some reassurance in my disidentification from being the one who falls apart or lets her down by being "just sexual." She seemed to confirm this in the next session, noting she felt "not guilty" about the sexual issue and glad that clear bounds had been set. Interestingly, I did not actually know the details of my analyst's and my friend's relationship. What may have been more important was getting to the fantasy of incest, and to the accompanying anger (and jealousy) with the idealized mentor. These feelings and processes would have relevance to F's situation *and* mine. In incest fantasy there are various painful but developmentally necessary wounds to self-esteem and/or idealization; in actual incest there is a direct wound to the core self, a violation. F too seemed to be getting to a similar realization in the dream.

37.

Transference	*Countertransference*
F said she wanted to do some work with another, female analyst. [This analyst had recently become my personal analyst.]	*I wondered again if F was psychic, or unconsciously trying to lead me to what I (or she?) needed – namely, a better connection to . . .*
She saw this female analyst as an "Earth Goddess" and me as "her consort."	*. . . the Feminine, or a Good Mother? Being linked on equal terms with my analyst made me feel a little better.*
"There's no danger of you not respecting her. I imagine you being able to honor her."	*However, I also felt less competent, competitive and afraid I'd lose F to her. [I advised against F's idea for now, "maybe later."]*

Discussion

This patient had an uncanny knack, or so it seemed, for getting me into awkward, confusing situations. Even if I had felt that simultaneous "multiple analyses" were fruitful, which I did not, this predicament would have been impossible. There was a sense of F either leading me or following in my footsteps. Either way, here was another incestuous, rivalrous triangle in the transference/countertransference. This one seemed to have a prospective aspect as well in her fantasy of a female/male syzygy (with special emphasis on the feminine). The problem, as usual, was that the patient was so close to home that I was threatened, and had to struggle with it.

38. Patient's dream

I've found a 3½-year-old girl walking in the city, abandoned by her parents. I'm in [hometown] with my family in the dark. I leave in a car, too fast, then on a bike to see you and [the female analyst]. Driving, I realize there are 3 or 4 kids and a baby in my arms in back. I better get up front. I have to hold the baby and drive.

I get there, feeling like a refugee. The first appointment is with her, but the building's burned down. My feeling is it's more important to see you. She takes me and my husband to your office.

Countertransference

At the time I felt relatively reassured about my decision to discourage her simultaneously seeing my analyst. I noted after session that F tended to project that helpless, incompetent "refugee" onto men, and that I was certainly prone, as in this instance with my analyst, to experience just that. I fantasized that the age of her "wounded child" in this dream jibed nicely with a particular emotional issue of my own at that age. I therefore wrote:

"You get the patients you need," as they say in Zurich, and how. Love/hate. Feel pretty smart and then they take you to another level of need for analysis. I'll have to have my vulnerability out there where she can really stomp on it – [is this] parallel to her own acting out toward her child self?

This is what it's like to be her (syntonic countertransference)?

Discussion

Though it is not a direct path, over time one can see the counter-transference deepening and regressing alongside the patient's unconscious. My fantasies, feelings and "countertransference neurosis" had more or less followed a line from adult-romantic to teen love to incest questions to these earlier separation issues. Of course this was only one line of several that could be described, and which surfaced, as did the transference, in a complicated mixture.

39. Patient's dream

You have a totem animal, a fox, and a 10-year-old son. There is a female assistant with you who's kind of neutral, like a eunuch, not much personality.

You and she told my husband and me we won't be able to get ferns until August. The woman said, "You can still plant them, but in smaller pots." I thought, "There's no reason why we need to wait." You asked, "Would you like to talk?" I feel this intense "air problem."

76

Countertransference

I'd been going through much doubt about my (in)abilities, especially compared to the superior "feminine" qualities that F had seemed to be seeking in my analyst. So this vision of a bland female side hurt some. I was not surprised, though, as I figured F would see me as heartless, as usual, and she did say "eunuch" with what felt like a special, perhaps retaliatory vigor. I did worry I was suffocating her, while trying to rationalize that the dream assistant only asked her to wait a bit.

Discussion

The decision to analyze rather than act out is often hard to maintain under patient and countertransference pressure. She perhaps perceived me as sly (like a fox), my female side as deficient, and my delaying tactics as smothering. What F needed, a life-giving connection to the feminine (internally and via the transference), was certainly not an inappropriate longing. In my experience (and maybe in hers) I was not only the rigid father but the inadequate mother with whom such a less than optimal feminine identification had taken place.

40. Countertransference dream

I'm showing F my cane fly rod. I explain to her its "classic" line and beauty. She doesn't understand the casting – I explain that you cast the line over and over again: "That's the beauty of it."

[My associations: the rod was a gift from my late father, whose father had given it to him – a much valued inheritance, traditional in the best sense. Phallic but fluid. The patient repetition of fly-fishing reminded me of analysis.]

Discussion

The therapist's dreams can have not only an explanatory but a compensatory effect upon the analytic situation. This one seemed to confirm, as I saw it objectively, the value of my more "classic" approaches to analysis in general and to the recent frame/boundary problems with F and my analyst in particular. Subjectively, for me, it suggested a growing connection and dialogue between male/female, logos/eros, new/old. This in turn was possibly apropos to F's self-described male/female "dichotomies" or "divinities." In these states of symbiosis or projective identification and counteridentification, it may be difficult to say whether analyst is preceding patient or vice versa, and whether standard sequential paradigms can explain the phenomenology.

41. Countertransference fantasy

I became aware for the first time of something sexual in my feelings for my daughter, then only six months old. Since I adored her, I felt deeply ashamed. I then was able to say to myself: Well, sexual curiosity and even something like a sexual impulse can and do exist between fathers and their infant daughters.

Discussion

And *love* of any sort may be coupled with some urge to concretize it, sexually or otherwise. In the case of incestuous feelings, the love expresses itself in *not* being concretized, that is, in being sacrificed. Vis-a-vis my patient all this helped me to realize that the distinction I'd been struggling with between sexual and non-sexual love was less self-evident than I had thought. Searles, speaking of "Oedipal Love in the Countertransference," expresses this aptly:

> the beloved parent reciprocates his [the child's] love – responds to him, that is, as being a worthwhile and lovable individual, as being, indeed, a conceivably desirable love-partner – and renounces him only with an accompanying sense of loss on the parent's own part. The renunciation is, I think, again something which is a mutual experience for child and parent, and is made in deference to a recognizedly greater limiting reality.
>
> (Searles, 1959, p. 296)

42. Patient's dream

Two female therapists, who work for you or something, are trying to tell me the analysis with you is going to terminate – it's done, I'm better. They put huge mirrors on either side of me.

I ask, "Is it time for me to go?" One woman says, "Yeah, now we're mixing higher and lower functioning people" and I'm one of the lower functioning ones. I start to protest, but the idea is they are normal and I'm not.

I leave, feeling like a refugee. It's the end of therapy and I'm sad and despondent. My husband says, "You have his briefcase." I'm thinking of a replacement.

Countertransference reflections

Pondering this and similar of F's "dreams of me with woman auxiliaries," I wrote:

She was seeing a neutered, sexless feminine in me. Yet could I let her be the anima-enhancer; do I need to let her cure me before or to cure herself? Or do I just contain it quietly or interpret back to her?

A kind of dynamic tension between her push/pull bodily toward me and my showing her [in the fly rod dream] the classic line (patriarchal, to be sure).

[The expressive work F had requested] is limited by my general style, my supervisors, ethics, the sexual transference/countertransference, and her needs (stated by her and perceived by me) for me to not break the bounds.

(Tempted to break bounds?) Yes and no. Fantasies about showing myself off as a "hipster"-swinger, dressing cooler. No: not really, not really worth it, not that enraptured. A fantasy thing really. Not compelled also by my deeper and growing concern for her "child" – abandoned, incestuously threatened – much like my own positively sexual, but bounded feelings for [my daughter].

Discussion

At the same time as I in my reflections deepen my capacity to "see" the child, or her as child, F in her dream is experiencing child-like abandonment and rejection feelings. (The latter may have been exacerbated by my cautions, both appropriate and self-serving, about her diluting her analysis with me, which resulted in an unconscious perception that I was uninterested in her "lower-functioning" aspects.) If there is a necessary fusion between analyst and patient, then what the analyst can feel and see in himself – that is, in his own "inner patient" or wounded side – may begin to correspond to a development or potential development in the client. In this case, my growing vision and awareness of sacrifice may correspond to her own growing potential not to attack her own inner child, a movement from the negative, incestuous father-animus to a more kindly one.

43.

Transference	*Countertransference*
F spoke of her relations with men: "trading sex for holding . . . then I'd be entitled to it [the holding]."	What I had been resisting – this trading on her beauty. I wondered further about incest.
She had imagined peeling her father off her back, "like skin." This left raw skin on which she placed butterflies.	Bambi. Childlike and kind of sweet, but it seemed to me a little corny and contrived.
F reported that a growth group leader had invited her to do individual work. She had also once been F's supervisor.	I felt angry; a reprise of the situation with my analyst? [I said, "I have the fantasy of you running away and each time I bring you back."]
F spoke throughout with a cavalier, "laughing it off" quality.	I felt tired of this and remarked that this style was "painful" and "irritating."

Discussion

The patient's further realizations and images, in this case of the sexualization of her dependency needs, become more clear to her in fairly direct succession to the analyst's seeing more clearly. My more open responses may indicate not just increasing freedom within the countertransference due to recent work, or me as the too-close father – they also show me trying to "catch" that defended or runaway child and "hold" her to her feelings. This in essence would be the opposite of abandoning her, or letting her abandon me. Not letting her ditch me is, in turn, a syntonic and perhaps prospective/corrective countertransference position: F felt abandoned as a child and unconsciously felt or wanted to say, "You can't leave me like this." The analyst, deeply fused, may have reactions the client might have and/or might identify with.

44. Countertransference reflections

Talking about *rage, what about* feeling *it?*

– detachment tempers or eliminates rage.

My sense: due to countertransference, her rage will wound me? Her sense intuitively is similar? Therefore, when I can bear it, she will let me have it [anger]?

More and more, the sexual countertransference = as a bridge to deeper, real relationship. If this woman wanted to go to bed with me, I'd be tempted but I wouldn't.

Discussion

The countertransference continues to cycle around to the erotic side, and I worry about how my narcissistic vulnerabilities might limit her growth. This is an attempt to get my feelings out of the way, based on an understanding that her narcissistic "radar" is such that she might repress her needs in order to take care of mine – a repeat of the pattern with the fragile, incestuous father and deteriorated mother.

Thus an analyst makes an attempt to not repeat the pathology by analyzing it: in himself, in the area of apparent fusion of his wounds with the patient's, and finally in the patient separately. In addition to the benefits of non-repetition, there is the potential in these efforts by the therapist for a "corrective emotional experience" for the patient.

45. Countertransference dream

I'm at F's house, though it resembles mine. We are lovers and it's a blue, rainy-day, Sunday feeling. It's late and I should go soon – what if her husband returns?!

A courtesy van comes down the driveway and the guy hooks a cable around this gigantic tree to tow it. The tree is deeply notched and huge. He chainsaws it some more and I worry it'll fall on the house. It doesn't, to my relief.

I worry about the whole thing: her husband, lawsuits, the end of our relationship, what my analytic society will say (how can you do analysis with her, having slept with her?)

Feeling tender and sad, I tell her I'll be going today. I lay my hand on her chest, then maybe on her shoulders.

Discussion

It was as if F and I had been having an affair – or an "analytic marriage" – for these many months. Insofar as this dream related to the countertransference relationship, the recently emerging idea of *sacrifice* is now introduced, or reiterated, at the unconscious level. It had always been around on the conscious level, as I struggled to contain my side of the erotic situation. The phallic tree and the fantasy relationship were impressive but, like my incestuous feelings toward my daughter, they rightly had to be sacrificed. This would appear to be (or need to be) in progress, with an appropriately deep sense of mourning (and the help of the tree service – amusing touch, that). The countertransference relation now is moving to a new phase.

46.

Transference	Countertransference
In a complex chain of events, F failed to call to confirm a session and arrived after I'd gone home. I got a message from her the next day.	*I worried she'd feel abandoned and called her as soon as possible. I felt genuinely sorry, though not guilty, that the time got "disorganized."*
Processing in session, F said she'd fantasized, "You would know I was coming, so I wouldn't have to call."	*I had waited awhile, and even called her home before leaving. I had imagined she'd fantasize this way.*

Discussion

A small, active demonstration of empathy – my calls – that I might not have made earlier. Likewise, I could anticipate and accept her dependency and omnipotent, narcissistic expectations, as I was less under her "spell" and more in an adaptive position.

47.

Transference	Countertransference
F's father had been on TV, and she'd fantasized calling to tell me. She thought, "He'd remind you of me."	I thought, "Wow, famous father!" I enjoyed this fantasy of connection with a celebrity.
F was "proud but I don't want you to think I like him. His fame is at my expense."	She and I are both enjoying the idea of her semi-famous father, but then she breaks it off.
Later F asked, "What's your Ph.D. in?"	I felt defensive – a "quality check"? I'm a Ph.D., like Dad? She wants to be an analyst and is getting degree information?

Discussion

Here the analyst again anticipates and then shares the early idealization of the father. This empathic position allows the patient to admit her own proud connection and identification, followed quickly by her disillusionment. There is then an apparent attempt to re-create or repair the narcissistic wound through an identification with a new idealized "Ph.D.", whom she may now want to be "just like" (according to the countertransference fantasy). The therapist may have to move rapidly within his evolving countertransference feelings, in order to be able to meet or "incarnate" a narcissistic transference (e.g. on the "Ph.D." thing I could move from self-doubt, to identity with Dad, to seeing her need for a reparative merger with me).

48. Countertransference dream (night before session)

I'm lying in our bedroom with my wife, and F lies to the left of her. F has slightly graying hair. It feels like she is part of the "family."

Transference	Countertransference
We started late, causing F to have fantasies of my not being there. She had often arrived a bit late to avoid just this thing, she said.	I'd had a crisis call but didn't mind making her wait, rationalizing it against her chronic lateness.

Coupling this with a recent miss (section 46), F saw me changing from being need-fulfilling to unreliable.

I'd made a large, empathic effort on that occasion, so this felt like straight projection.

She wanted me to give her a "5-minute" warning before the end of session. [I did so].

I thought, "It's hard for her to stop, not just start, sessions." Dependency risks?

She had fantasies of being able to call me at home, but didn't want to "interfere" with my wife and family.

I thought immediately of my dream, and noted my importance to her and her need for a mirroring "availability."

Discussion

While this dream suggested on the objective level that F might be "interfering" (as she feared) with my family life, it also signalled the possibility that I could be more "available" to her emotional "call" (as she synchronistically requested that very day). The dream – especially its feeling tone – imaged an intimate, "familiar" relationship and that image/feeling allowed me to bring the necessary availability of feeling to her in session. Whatever F represented to me subjectively was closer to home. As I integrated this internal F into my inner "family," so to speak, the outer F's needs did not seem so much like "interference" to me, her or my marriage. I was better able to respond to her needs in session (the 5-minute warning, the mirroring) rather than get hung up on whether to let her call me at home (see section 19, p. 57). This dream and the emotional movements in the ensuing hour follow a line of thought emphasized a month before in the preceding countertransference dream (section 45, pp. 81–82) – towards the "affair" being over.

49. Patient's dream

Sitting with me is [former therapist], who is also you. I have a feeling of warmth, safety, and comfort. Protected.

He's sitting in his car, going away. I say, "Can I go with you? . . . I'm just joking." He moves over to let me in the driver's seat.

[Associations: she "resisted" the chance to work through her father's "leaving" with this therapist, who terminated prematurely. Control issues: driver vs. passenger? . . . "I'm feeling more trust, closeness, *serenity, like eating something delicious. . . . But I don't want you to feel good about that . . . I can feel a tiny little bit of feeling sorry for my father; I identified with him for a second."]*

Discussion

This dream was also in response to an upcoming vacation break, which seemed to echo previous "leavings." The recent deepening of her dependency and trust seems evident, though F maintains the cautious capacity to "laugh it off," if necessary. Relations to "father," whom I was undoubtedly carrying and embodying, show some improvement, perhaps in tandem with my own slight improvements.

50. Patient's dream

My sister and I are in bed. Dad wants us to read his book, which is split in half. I'm trying to tell him I don't like his style. I'm comparing it to another book, The Mists of Avalon. *He may be kind of miffed.*

Transference	Countertransference
[I asked her, "What about my style?"]	Feeling more daring.
F then criticized my "workaholism, neglect of the child that wants to play, intimacy problems and neglect of family and spouse."	She didn't sugar-coat it, but neither did I feel all of this was exactly true of me. It really didn't click, though I considered it.
F spoke of her father's "never at a loss" persona.	I'd felt compelled to appear that way with her.
She added her growing disrespect for various men at work, who had "never been in therapy . . . I can't trust them or look up to them . . . they're cut off from huge areas of themselves."	I felt some relief – figuring she must have known that I had been in analysis. I was glad these guys were getting it, not me.
Men, like her husband, appeared to be "strong, completely together, no cracks," – then she'd find these "incredible weaknesses."	I was always a bit afraid to let her down and apprehensive about what "incredible weaknesses" she'd see in me.

She'd like to have the power to "make men into slaves."	*She wasn't far from having that, as I knew firsthand.*

Discussion

There is a kind of voluntary joining with the patient's transference here, based on the dream imagery. Increasingly, with greater comfort with the countertransference positions, the therapist can let himself imagine that various images refer to him. Whether they do or not, they can then be brought into the therapy situation. The patient's disappointment in a lack of feminine relatedness (in others and in the transference), and the disdain and power demands that result, are pretty evident. To be on the receiving end of this, embodying in the countertransference successive states of strength and collapse, can be difficult.

51. Patient's dream

I'm in a natural foods store where I hear my father laugh. What's he doing here? I leave to avoid him.

He's unbuttoning the top button of what I'm wearing in a way that's motherly, jerky and efficient, not sexual. He gives us [family] a chocolate Valentine heart, in a gentle, giving way that's shy and unsure.

In a hotel now, we're going to leave my daughter with him and his ex-wife, about which I feel doubts. He has tweed pants on, though, with Sesame Street characters on them! My daughter is all over them. It's OK to play and fool around.

[Associations: F saw her father's book in a bookstore. She felt proud and wanted to tell me, though also "ashamed of being proud." She said, "I can't stand the thought of anything around my neck . . . . Stifled . . . . Like what you wear."]

Discussion

Recent work is apparently bearing fruit, as we see the image of the "good father" more clearly established and at work (or play) in her. The scene is reminiscent of the time F actually brought her daughter into session (section 29, pp. 65–66). The level of trust of her "little girl" seems to have expanded considerably, as has the level of trustworthiness in the transference.

52. Countertransference dream

With my wife and others I am saying goodbye to F. There is a question about revealing things, like my own children. I fill up a canister of grain to the top – for her children.

Discussion

It looked like, in terms of F as patient, the sacrifice of the huge tree (see section 45, pp. 81–82) and the countertransference containment were now bearing fruit, too. The old tree went down, but here were the seeds of growth for her development (her children). The harvest was in. This is my gift to her. Prospectively, this dream seemed to point to the "affair" aspect being transformed, to the achievement at a real emotional level of her goal: wanting me to fall in love with her but needing me not to. As with the patient's dreams and fantasies, the therapist's countertransference will hopefully indicate a progression, not only of his own growth but of his growth in conjunction with the patient's.

53. Patient's dream

I'm in the audience watching a short, dark, narcissistic man on a table.

Then I'm in session with you. You seem like [the actor] William Hurt – big, soft, safe, maternal, confident. I'm sitting on the floor with my head in your lap, docile, like a young girl.

The tyrant had been locked up, and went crazy because he was losing his charisma. The sense was people were cajoling him, but not confronting him.

Our session ended abruptly. The tyrant realized the truth, no longer hidden from him. I don't feel bad because you go out to help him. I go with you. You're doing it but I'm with you.

Discussion

Nice imagery here as patient and therapist go off together to deal firmly with the tyrannical narcissistic problem. Two quotes from Jung seem appropriate, the first related to this specific session and the ongoing analytic engagement, the second to the aptly named image of the therapist, Dr. "Hurt:"

Where love reigns, there is no will to power; and where the
will to power is paramount, love is lacking.

(Jung, 1943, p. 53)

It is no loss either if he feels the patient is hitting him, or
even scoring off him: it is his own hurt that gives the measure of his power to heal. This, and nothing else, is the
meaning of the Greek myth of the wounded physician.

(Jung, 1951a, p. 116)

CASE TWO: MS. J

J was an abuse victim – raped by a babysitter at age 7 – with
severe weight problems. Her parents reportedly being unem-
pathic, she did not mention the rape to anyone until her 20s. J's
relationship with her father was emotionally incestuous (actual
incest was denied, though its intimation made J very anxious).
Mother was dependent and "nice." J was the eldest of her siblings, who were married, unlike her. She felt herself to be an
outsider in the family, and her sense of alienation carried over to
her work life, where she had resigned or been fired from jobs at
regular, approximately yearly intervals. She presented with
impulsive suicidal ideation, a history of past attempts, and an
extensive but reportedly unsatisfactory therapy history.

Course of treatment and countertransference

The initial countertransference experience with Ms. J was almost
entirely different from that with the previous patient, Ms. F.
While I was favorably predisposed toward F, with J my
inclination was to withdraw. If the term were in use (in the way
one refers to transferences), it would be accurate to call mine a
"negative countertransference" to J. This was not a matter of
dislike, but rather of a lack of a positive draw. "Resistance"
would be the more correct term. I anticipated difficulty.

However, while the projected analytic relationship appeared
less inviting than with an "attractive" patient, the countertransference process was in other ways similar. In fact the difficulty in
forming a non-combative linkage between us was the crux of the
transference/countertransference, and of J's history, as might be
guessed. J's case, which will be presented without the point-by-

point detail of the previous one, will show that a negative countertransference can be as engaging and informative as a positive one, and equally subject to transformation.

1. J's suicidal ideation and a possibly borderline quality put me emotionally on guard from the beginning. Objectively, suicide seemed unlikely once she had established contact and contracted with me, and admitted her disappointed anger at the previous therapist who had referred her to me. But J did have a volatile history in this regard and others. I did not like her impulsive way of doing things, however unconscious, and did not like the tense atmosphere that surrounded her.

Accordingly, I was tentative about committing myself to working with her. In response to her questions about insurance, I told her I did not know if our sessions would be covered. I spoke with her ex-therapists about diagnosis, history and suicidality. I questioned her closely about her present suicidal feelings. I eventually said I would see her only if she would agree to twice-weekly sessions. I felt she would need at least this frequency and, incidentally, that I would too – both to keep track of her and, frankly, to be well paid for it.

Meanwhile, J was equally and perhaps appropriately cautious about me. She told me in our first hour she didn't want therapy now or to become a "professional patient." She said she could not afford the fee. She cancelled the second session by phone, until she could find out more about her insurance coverage.

Discussion

The patient wants and needs a commitment to the process, though herself uncommitted, but the therapist at first may not be ready to give it. There appears to be a matching ambivalence and resistance about starting up. Conditions are sometimes set by the therapist not simply because they are clinically appropriate, but because they are reassuring to him. There is also a somewhat mercenary and compensatory component in this particular countertransference, on the order of: If I'm going to take on a demanding patient, I expect at least to be financially rewarded. Thus my first fantasies were of being depleted.

Behind all this, the main feature is the early struggle around analytic "engagement." In my experience this takes place *every* time when working from a countertransference position. In contrast to the situation with patient F, the problem here is being "under-engaged" (though in another sense "overengaged" with anxieties about J, some objective and some subjective). Because this way of working means becoming "involved" with the patient – "infected" – the therapist at the unconscious level may be subject to anxieties about separation, immersion and/or abandonment. These worries play themselves out at the start of treatment and may be especially relevant to the "characterological" condition that J presented. Without denying the analyst's need for a private working through, this kind of ambivalence and "distrust" in the countertransference can also be used as a barometer of the client's own anxiety level around intimacy. At this point there is a coalescence of neurotic, concordant and complementary counter-transferences, waiting to be sorted out and/or lived through.

2. It was more than J's diagnosis, depression or volatility that raised my anxiety with her. Concerns about these were relatively conscious. Putting aside words and trying to receive her without preconceptions, I found her manner and her whole "being" un-settling. My first sight of J was of her trying to cool off by sitting on the inside steps of my office building. It was summer, but this unconventional waiting room behavior made me uneasy. Nor did she look at me much. Eye contact is overrated, but she seemed distracted and brooding. While J's weight surely contributed to the ruminating quality, her size per se did not put me off excess-ively. Rather, the connective difficulty seemed to arise from the mass of her steamy, unsettled vibrations – she was like a frustrated child, about to blow. J later confirmed this, saying she felt like a "bomb" about to go off.

Discussion

Though the above description may sound unsympathetic, none-theless the therapist's "experience" of the patient can comple-ment a more refined, intellectual assessment. This experiential impression is essentially the analyst's non-verbal, feeling response to the patient's own non-verbal style: what she looks like and does, "how" she says it, etc. All this is what the patient "is" to him, so far, not what he thinks she is. It is what the patient "is" in the analyst's unconscious.

For instance, the first patient, F, was seen initially as a kind of romantic, "Psyche"-like goddess; very pleasant, full of erotic potential. With J, however, I was experiencing and imaging someone, or even some-"thing," difficult to empathize with. My own jungle-like, primitive images of her and apprehensive feelings were probably constellated by the primitive affective states (and marginal defenses) she was bringing into the emotional field.

All this comes through a countertransference process that is "primitive" itself, but only in the best sense of that word. It is also often termed "primary process," which is not inaccurate but carries a slightly unsophisticated connotation. This kind of sensing of the patient is potentially quite refined and forms a tangible basis and reference point for anything one can secondarily process, interpret or say. It is a process before words, but without which words have no "felt" meaning[4]. It may also be the psychological space where emotional change actually occurs. Thus the primitive and primary form the basis for the primacy of the countertransference.

3. Though furtive and seemingly out of contact with me, J nevertheless had her eyes and ears on me. Evidently her agitated presentation was not only because she had much to say, but because she expected it to go unheard. In fact on one level she *insisted* on being seen, and watched me like a hawk to see if I was doing it correctly. Her radar was sharp: if I averted my glance, she thought I was bored or tired; if I checked the clock, she would notice. This did not quite paralyze me; but her perceptions of my lack of interest left her in an irritable state. At this point attempts to interpret this had no effect on her basic sense that I "didn't care." She was in effect serving notice about what she demanded – perfect mirroring – while also insisting that I was not providing it. This then gave her the opportunity to open up her attacks on me personally for such empathic failures.

Discussion

A patient in this state, with a tenuous working alliance and a deprivational history, may not respond to interpretation. Interpretation does not matter, or mean anything. The transference is simply "in effect." A test is given, proof is required. What seems to be needed is a lengthy struggle to establish trust on the primary "experiential" level noted above. The analyst and analytic situation must disprove the past, somehow. At this apparently infantile or "primitive" level, an interpretation may not fit the need, except insofar as the patient may hear at least that the therapist is thinking about her (or may respond to the sound of his voice). This, however, is usually not "good enough," as the dissatisfaction cannot be assuaged.

4. J, the other therapists, the multiple sessions and the pay- ments had reassured me sufficiently to lean toward working with her. Despite her own ambivalence, she had been eager to know if I would continue to see her. She helped my decision along when she said her "gut feeling" was that she felt "comfortable enough" with me, and when she apologized to me for being a "bear," as she put it. Though compliant perhaps, she was not oblivious to her effects on people, and to *my* security needs. She said, "I don't know if you want to work with me because I'm so angry."

Discussion

Here is another very perceptive patient. J was enough of a care-taker to intuitively sense my discomfort and try to make it better. In the complicated "trust" dance between us, it was as if we struck a non-therapeutic bargain: I would work with her if she didn't frighten me *too* much. Narcissistically wounded herself, her nose for others' distress was acute. But it was this "attention" to others (and to me) that had to go, so she could express her resentment. It soon went.

5. Though now less fearful she would suicide, I started to become physically scared of J, who outweighed me by one hundred pounds. She mentioned her anger at the previous therapists, which I presumed to be a reference to me or my implicit hesitations about her. J then described how she had wanted to "choke" me: once when I had not reassured her about insurance coverage, once when I apologetically said I could not read a giant stack of important, old letters she presented, and another time when she read an article on rape (a subject she was very frightened of). She said this – "I want to choke you!" – with a certain amount of conviction.

J also reported in one session four dreams about me:

1. *You were sitting still at one end of a swimming pool bench and I was trying to slide away on the other.*
2. *You had other patients and I was "not special."*
3. *I wanted to choke you and push you off a cliff.*
4. *I hit you.*

All this in combination with the brooding intensity of these earlier sessions caused me alarm. I had some fretful fantasies centering around "control" and limit-setting and how to handle pressures on the frame or phone calls at home. I noted after one meeting, "I felt *very* sleepy this session. Significant material?" I made interpretive efforts about her approach-avoidance behavior (trust → fear → breaking off), which relieved neither her nor me. I thought (to myself) that she felt rage towards me either because I was a man, hence not to be trusted (incestuous father, rapist?), or an unreceptive, unprotective mother.

Discussion

Again, we were not in an interpretive situation, though the dreams, for example, showed an interesting sequence of fear of intimacy, narcissistic injury, retaliation and anger. While the approach-avoidance behavior is clearly not just J's, she is evidently as scared of me as I am of her (more so in fact). There is a considerable amount of meaningful material here, and her aggressive reaction to unmet need is quite understandable. But the rather unmodified expression of hostility in a negative transference causes a countertransference resistance, leading to potential withdrawal and loss of empathy. So together we were in a "mutual resistance." While such shared resistances are probably unfortunate and unprogressive, they are almost unavoidable with patients experienced (by me at least) as difficult. Moreover, the working through of such mutual distrust can in itself become the keynote of the healing process.

6. Nevertheless, alongside her aggressive feelings J, on occasion, would suddenly express very concrete, "loving" ones. In the (mostly rare) moments when she became convinced of my having understood her, she wanted to "hug" me. Though J did not hug me, I would tend to feel relieved by this expression, as it let me off the hostility hook and seemed genuine, not a reaction formation. But the rapid fluctuations and the sheer physicality of her desire, even if they were toward the "positive" side, *also* made me anxious. I feared J was either going to clobber me, or leap up and crush me – without much notice either way.

Discussion

A "resistance to fusion" with patients may come not just from fear of being attacked but from fear of being batted around in crazy, oscillating feeling states. This is fear of being "con-*fused*." It is also what Jung calls the "atmosphere of illusion" or "fog," what Searles calls the "ambivalent symbiosis," and Goodheart calls (after Langs) the "complex-discharging field." J's first dream of the analysis had touched on these interactive fields of mutual and confused identity:

I'm sitting at dinner at my grandmother's house. I've served chocolate ice cream to her, my sister and mother, but there's no bowl for me.

I have to have a bowel movement but it's for my grandmother. When I come back, my sister is cleaning off my grandmother like she'd done it. There's a pile of b.m. in the kitchen. I left a pile in the other room.

I look for more ice cream, but they'd ate it all, and seconds. I clean up both poops. I started crying and feel like a handmaiden, like Cinderella.

Thus J's aforementioned boundary problems with father extended as or more deeply to other, female family members. The unconscious tendency to get into pathologically symbiotic relationships was apparently being reenacted with me and I, like her, tended to feel swamped by it.

7. J's deprived, undernourished feeling and consequent rage now came close to the surface. In one session she dropped the crucial letters (see p. 92), from which I had gently suggested she pick out important ones, and almost exploded. She marched to the window; she wanted to throw her keys at me. I wasn't sure if she would jump out, or jump me. I may have asked her to sit down. In other sessions she had fantasies of "busting up" my office, breaking chairs and tearing my pictures and books off the walls. I was definitely worried she would act out (or act in), and aware that, if push came to shove, she was considerably larger than I was. I tried a blend of casualness and understanding, "I really don't go for that [breaking my furniture], but I can understand your anger about things." This comment seemed sort of vapid to me, but was the best I could do. There was enough residual ego there that she could control, or felt she should control, her anger.[5]

Discussion

The need to discharge becomes so strong here that the therapeutic vessel or *temenos* is threatened, as well as the therapist's sense of well-being. This again is part of the long test – to hold without withdrawing or retaliating. I was having trouble being "with" J when she wanted to destroy me. Yet these destructive feelings had to become acceptable in some way to me (and hence J). Failing that, she might experience a (non-)therapeutic repeat of the mother who reportedly could only tolerate "nice" things or might vaporize under her attacks.

8. Aspects of J's relationship with father now began to surface in important ways. In terms of the countertransference I found myself one day realizing that, whenever I thought of the "rape," I had it mixed up with "incest" in my mind. An important part of an early dream, along with the reported history, had cued this:

I'm in the second bedroom with Dad, close but not touching, talking. I hear Mom coming and yell down and joke, "We're playing the 'Sex and Marriage' game." Mom is surprised. I tell her it's a joke. I say, "We haven't done anything – ask Dad." Dad doesn't say anything.

J forcefully denied any incest, though she revealed some very suspicious boundary violations between him, her and others. She was aware of her strong attachment to her father. I was aware of a rather shocked reaction on my part to her father's and mother's alleged *lack* of reaction to J's rape. Under the circumstances I expressed some of my incredulity to J, especially as among her basic experiences in life were a lack of mirroring and emotional validation – leading to the feeling that nobody "believed" her. I also voiced criticism of her father's "confusing" (to her and to the "little girl" in her) boundary distortions.

Discussion

In my opinion there are times, with a rape or possible incest victim who has had baffling or toxic parental reaction (or lack of reaction), when a "corrective" empathic response from the therapist is called for. Hopefully, this models a more healthy emotion, and defends the germ of a true self driven into hiding. Because it will "lead" the patient, however, the therapist's use of a strong countertransference reaction needs to be checked closely for its sincerity and displacement value. In this case the situation was multi-determined: my criticisms were essentially appropriate and came from an outraged place in me where she was my daughter (a "corrective" complementary countertransference, so to speak). But in addition they were also partly to deflect J's angry frustrations from me (and/or mine from her). That is: she hits me, I hit *them* (instead of her, possibly, or to distract her from me). It is considerably easier to embody positive, "caring" countertransference positions than angry, destructive ones. The latter are not only uncomfortable but may also interfere with the therapist's self-image, fantasy or persona as an empathic person.

9. As the work progressed, J sheepishly admitted her graphic sexual fantasies about me. Transference dreams – one where she dismembered a devilish, father-like man; another where a man in a white lab coat (a "Doctor," like her father or me) threatened to kill her – had already made me wonder about my own hostile feelings, not just hers. Was my anger: induced (by her projective identification), self-protective, resistant, natural, all of the above? As I struggled with this, I was surprised to have a countertransference dream on the other side of things:

I've got a musty, country cottage. I'm in bed at one point with J. She's somewhat near to me.

J talks about [an airline pilot I knew], who's been coming down on weekends to give her "psychoanalytic instruction." I feel this can't hurt. I think: this guy, a pilot, must have really changed to be in analysis.

She's been looking at some of my stuff on my desk, sees her name on a desk pad or list, and asks about it. I don't feel threatened by her curiosity, but I do growingly feel this whole deal is too close a situation. In fact, is it ethical? I'm about to tell her, though she just moved in, that she'll have to move out.

As I'm about to, I see a neighbor, whom I heard earlier in the house. He's doing something about the heating.

J gets in a big fight with this neighbor's cohort, who wears glasses. I hear him yell at J, at one point in total but controlled rage. He then comes by me and half-smilingly says, "Don't want to miss a good fight."

I fold up a mildewed sheet as I think, "I'll have to move from here" and wonder, indeed, "How did I get here . . . . What am I doing in this second house?" "What'll my wife think?"

Discussion

This dream recalls one with the previous client, F (p. 81), and also bore a general correspondence to J's dream (section 8, pp. 95–96) where she and father are playing the "sex and marriage" game. Among the complications of countertransference-based work can be when it gets too fused for too long, and this had special relevance for this type of victimized client. I had of course experienced J as invasive (just as she experienced penetrative fears), and had withdrawn from or tried to control *her* at times (just as she did to me and others). But we were evidently closer than I had realized, and she was really "under my skin."

What about my end of it? The musty cottage recalled my childhood home and the sad, love/rage splitting therein and in me (not unlike J's, though less radical and better controlled). Accordingly, in the dream we appeared to be oscillating between too cold and too hot, which, again, was what I feared in her and what she feared in her feelings about and experience of males. I had not fully considered my anger at J nor certain personal/ historical aspects of it. Nor had I been aware of any possible attraction to her. This compensatory dream showed my struggle (and the need) for increased clarity on these topics and proper analytic limits. It would seem to recommend reflection on my seductive, intellectualizing, and even provocative sides, in an attempt to get the emotional atmosphere in the analysis better regulated. The thermostat needs adjusting, for the fire ("heating") which energizes the alchemical transformation has to be the correct temperature.

Yet, while the psychological container must be appropriate, there are inevitable interminglings of the personal histories of each participant in the *coniunctio*. The analyst must be drawn in – hooked.

10. Close on to the above countertransference dream, J reported strong urges to suck her thumb and the following dream:

I'm a dinosaur and laying a big white egg. I'm parts of both of them.

She thought this dream represented the "old me changing into the new . . . a good sign." I agreed, silently speculating on the primitive, archaic imagery of the level she was re-birthing at, and the regressed, non-human nature of her identity. This private self-creation seemed a more safe and suitable fusion than ones

97

with mother(s), father, or me. There appeared to have been a movement from the initial, negative fusion states and dream (see p. 94).

In the countertransference, meanwhile, I found myself feeling less threatened by this pre-historic "Big Mama" with the demanding transference, whom I'd feared would devour me, kill me or kill herself. Her fantasies of looking up my home address and looking for my house became more interesting than frightening. When she wanted me to come to hear her perform in public, I gently declined but could resonate freely with the idea and tell her I had seen the announcement about her performance. I began to "see" her differently in my mind's eye.

Discussion

A better balance in the therapist permits a freer sense of empathy and mirroring. There seemed to be something of a simultaneous movement here in patient and therapist: as she showed symbolic, inner signs of self-renewal, I was, in part due to my own self-analysis, able to experience her fantasies symbolically and not fearfully. That is, I was no longer afraid of her acting out her needy, enveloping or aggressive fantasies. There was also a sequential movement with paradoxically positive effect: as I, after my dream, clarified my side of the boundary, we could then merge more fully in fantasy. We were more able to work in the "secured-symbolizing" field Goodheart refers to.

11. This emerging countertransference capacity to be less embroiled and concretized – less stuck in primitive "participation mystique" really – continued to grow, though not without severe ups and downs. When J wanted to rip my plants out, I could fantasize with her about "uprooting" things or the "roots" of feelings that she (and I) wanted to see. Likewise, her fantasy attacks on my bookshelves yielded good symbolic material: for me about my possibly intellectual or doctrinaire viewpoints on her, and for her about her desire to "know," her demand to be seen as an individual, her envy, and her fear I would abandon her due to her "hopeless," borderline diagnosis.

Though J's outer life remained volatile, with job changes, accidents and losses, we struggled along. The desire to concretize anger did not give way and was in some ways embodied in the above externals, but simultaneously a less ambivalent symbiosis also pushed forward, also pressing for concretization. J secretly "enacted" the following dream, she later told me, by touching my jacket as I led her into my office:

You and I are standing outside a white church on Christmas morning. It's your office. You can't get in either.

Inside we hear laughing and clapping. You want to buy something, a drink. I buy a paper. I offer to hold your drink: am I "helping" again? Kindly, you gave me the drink and paper and opened the doors to the sanctuary.

As we wait to go in, there are strong parts of me (sic) touching you. We're deciding who's going to walk up and go in first. This is playfully done – comfortably, like friends, with laughter and gaiety. I woke up with tears in my eyes.

Discussion

Since there is, among other things in the sessions and dreams, less need to "help" the therapist, J's unconscious seems to move forward with this positive *coniunctio*/resurrection theme in the transference (her associations were to a "wedding" and "Easter"). There had been a significant movement in mutual trust, my former hesitations having approximately paralleled hers. A "safe" container may be as important for the analyst as for the patient, not only for the analyst's sake but because its growth in and of itself is healing. The mutual creation and entrance into the sanctuary (or *temenos*) is almost as much a goal as a prerequisite for analytic work. Life-giving waters – in the case of J's dream, tears of joy – can then flow from this shared psychospiritual "container."

12. As J and I remained mostly in this more comfortable, play- ful atmosphere, her dreams continued to be telling. In one she seemed to find a room of her own:

At my parents' house Mom leaves the kitchen and Dad and I argue. He says, "Get out."

I say, "I will, it's not like I need you. You've never been there. I don't want to see you until you can talk about me, not your work and everybody else."

I walk out and wonder what friend I can stay with. Then it dawns on me I have my own house.

In another dream J's chronic sense that "no one cares," at home or in the transference, seems evident, with particular regard to her femininity:

I'm riding a tractor, thinking about the prom and the dress Mom and I are going to go buy. I'm very excited!

With Mom, Dad and grandparents, I'm talking eagerly about the prom. They're not listening. I stop and feel annoyed.

In the unspoken countertransference to the first dream I felt supportive of her separation from the negative father and her realization of her own individuation. This came without strain; that is, from a position of neutrality. In the second dream I felt real sadness, in a syntonic countertransference to go with her understandable anger. Behind all her anger, I felt, were tears.

Not too long after this, I noticed in session that J's large size seemed to me not merely repulsive or overwhelming, but really rather magnificent. I saw her, for the first time, as a "goddess," the embodiment of a sort of Amazonian power. She seemed "great," a giant, not "fat." I was aware that others, like her apparently un-individuated mother, had relied on her "strength," but this more solid vision of J did not feel dependency-based in me.

Discussion

Compensatory images of growth, understanding and strength emerge in succession in patient and analyst. When the latter can truly "see" the patient's possibilities, this can be especially nourishing when the patient's unconscious is suggesting parallel possibilities. But this synchronistic "matching" cannot be faked, or even expected. It may come naturally out of the shared unconscious space analyst and patient "play" in. Something new, arising from the union in the transference/countertransference, emerges in the "feeling-image" the therapist has of the patient. Before, J seemed massively sick to me, all anxiety (which I, too, experienced with her). Over time there had gradually grown within me a picture of J's "great"-ness, her full-body wholeness, that could now be "real"-ized almost concretely in the countertransference. This was, furthermore, a very different vision of her body (and of her femininity) than she or I had had before.

13. The importance of J's being properly "seen" was crucially indicated in a subsequent dream:

I'm about 8–10 years old in a grade school play yard. With girlfriends in a circle yelling, "Murder, Rape, Robbery." When I hear "rape," I walk away, trying to conceal the pain in my groin.

I almost run into a man's shoes – Dad's. He takes my hand and chatters about our "move" that night. Because of my silence and limp, he asks about it. I tell him I tripped. He chatters on.

A teacher like Mrs. Z comes up and asks me, "What's wrong? You seem so sad." I want to tell her about the rape but can't. She doesn't believe me about the family harmony.

She watches me now as Mom and I sit. It's graduation. Mom had a big smile but says angrily, "Hold my hand!" The teacher sees this happening, though she can't hear Mom.

Discussion

Against a background of introjected parental neglect and neediness (and J's understandable distrust), J's need *and* potential for being seen are here further outlined. Her associations to "Mrs. Z" were highly relevant (especially, for instance, in light of the "prom" dream, section 12, p. 100): this young teacher kindly offered J nickels for pads when J began menstruating. To correct the pathological symbiosis with the inner parents required the kinds of self-correction and "seeing" of her (e.g. my spontaneous "goddess" vision above) that had recently been occurring in the countertransference. The image of "Mrs. Z" is a measure of this, as well as a fine-tuning from J's unconscious of what J specifically required in the analysis – namely, J needed to be seen, or "seen through" sometimes, even when she could not see herself or dare to say what she needed.

14. Such seeing calls for delicate judgments and responses – all of which impact or depend on the countertransference, some of which the therapist will "fail" at. For example, near the end of a vacation break of mine J phoned and wanted to see me ahead of schedule. She was very anxious over a threatened job loss. I mirrored her anxiety, internally judged she could wait, and could not schedule her in anyway (nor did I particularly want to, being still on vacation). A minor suicidal gesture resulted. The upshot of this, when we worked through its multiple aspects, was again that J needed me, like Mrs. Z in the dream, to anticipate the despair J could not directly express.

Similarly, as her basic needs to touch and be touched escalated, J did not quite see why I would not give her a "hug" in a friendly way. I could see her "need" for this, but gently refused for a variety of reasons. One, it somehow feels wrong to me to hug my patients. Two, I especially feel reluctant to hug patients who have been raped (or who, as J once did, feel the protective need to stand by the door). Three, there was the incestuous boundary problem with father. Four, I found that in the countertransference I did not really want to hug J.

Discussion

The analyst's participatory attempts to embody the "healing" potentials imaged in the patient's unconscious (e.g. Mrs. Z), walk the objective/subjective line. The analyst and analytic situation incarnate the patient's unconscious in a paradoxical way which is at once quite real but also "as if." The analyst tries to remember this, particularly when the patient cannot yet, or may never, understand. For patients, ultimately it may have to be like the song says: "You can't always get what you want," but [from the therapy] ". . . you get what you need." At the same time the analyst's failures are unavoidable, perhaps even necessary in some way. Small failures can be very positive if worked through, and some failures are phase-appropriate (Kohut's "transmutative internalizations"), provided the initial "good enough" holding (Winnicott) has been sufficiently established. The analytic engagement is the crucible in which all this is hammered out over a long period of time. For the analyst the countertransference leads the way in this process.

4

CONCLUSIONS

It is surprisingly difficult to find examples of what actually happens in countertransference states. The material presented in Chapter 3 is an attempt to demonstrate the phenomenology of countertransference – countertransference "from the inside out." In Jungian psychology (and even to some extent in the psycho-analytic literature) one looks in vain for the this kind of detailed discussion. Almost nowhere in the Jungian literature, for instance, can a personal recounting of a countertransference dream be found, except for Jung's oft-cited dream of the patient in the tower (Jung 1937, 1943, 1950, 1961a)[1]. In this instance Jung led the way and nobody followed. Imperfect as it (or the analytic work) may be, the previous chapter is the most extensive written docu-ment to date on the phenomenology of countertransference from a Jungian perspective[2].

This document is, of course, one Jungian's perspective, and this chapter will attempt to generalize that individual perspective by theorizing further about a countertransference-oriented way of working. It will put together more systematically the bits and pieces of countertransference detail and theory that composed the last one. First, a general theory of countertransference will be described, and then a countertransference processing "model" will be outlined. Finally, selected countertransference issues of general importance will be discussed.

A THEORY OF COUNTERTRANSFERENCE

The use of countertransference as a therapeutic instrument has undergone much change, in Jungian as in other analytic circles. Jungian trends were outlined in the literature review. It appears that Jung, by implication if not directly, was the first psycho-therapist to endorse the positive potential of countertransference as an analytic technique. This represents an appropriate and very "Jungian" (in the sense of having a prospective tendency) supplement to his being the first analyst to recommend required training analysis as a safeguard against countertransference's *negative* potential.

Unfortunately, as also noted earlier, Jung did not follow up on this aspect of his work. However, the slack in countertransference study was admirably picked up by Fordham and the London SAP group. Jungians who are interested in countertransference processes are very much in their debt. The wide range of possibilities within the Jungian view of the psyche has also given rise to the other different and dynamic perspectives described in the review. These theories are a boon to the countertransference theorist.

Like most other Jungian writers, my thoughts about counter-transference have been much influenced by psychoanalytic writers. Harold Searles' work has been particularly important to me (see Sedgwick, 1993). I value highly the ideas of Margaret Little and Lucia Tower, whose work, along with that of other female analysts like Heimann, Cohen and Weigert[3], blazed the trail with Searles and Heinrich Racker in the early 1950s. Also influential are the theories and deeply empathic spirit of Kohut and Winnicott, which have important countertransference implications. Langs' technique is important and thought-provoking.

In all analytic schools, there has been a trend toward recognition not just of the value of countertransference but also of "mutuality" in the analytic process. Jung, of course, opened the door to this dimension through his work on transference. Even Freud (whose references, incidentally, to the term he invented are almost as sparse as Jung's[4]) perhaps inadvertently encouraged countertransference usage. While carefully advising his famous neutrality model of "the surgeon, who puts aside all his feelings, even sympathy," Freud adds:

> [The analyst] must bend his own unconscious like a recep-tive organ towards the emerging unconscious of the patient, be as the telephone receiver to the disc. As the receiver transmutes the vibrations induced by the sound-waves back again into sound-waves, so is the physician's unconscious mind able to reconstruct the patient's unconscious, which

has directed his associations, from the communications derived from it.

(Freud, 1912, p. 122)

While this may speak more to empathy than what Freud saw as countertransference, it still leaves room for the subjective reaction as an informative, reconstructive device.

There has been vigorous countertransference debate amongst Freudians. Jungians have suffered less (but also benefitted less) from a global debate on the appropriateness of countertransference use, due to Jung's technical flexibility and, until recently, a general inattention by most "classical" Jungians to the topic. This is unfortunate, for a certain dynamic tension about the subject, collectively, mirrors the inner conflict the individual, countertransference-oriented analyst undergoes.

At any rate there has been a progression, as Fordham *et al.* (1974, p. ix) have discussed vis-a-vis London and Chapter 2 demonstrates here, from the earlier one-sided, transference-only focus to one where countertransference can be used therapeutically and in conjunction with transference developments. The threads of the Jungian countertransference "schools" all unite in this latter region of alchemical *coniunctio*. This book's perspective partakes of all of the threads, with greatest emphasis on certain aspects and modifications of the "wounded-healer" and "rain-maker" positions.

The necessity of "neurotic" countertransference

The question of "neurotic" vs. "useful" countertransference has always been paramount. It is possible, however, to shift the perspective slightly. Clearly this book rests on the idea that counter-transference is useful in and for therapy. To make use of this potential, a first step is often made to divide countertransference into the discrete entities, "neurotic" and "useful." This is a natural and clinically necessary tendency; indeed it is always an important part of the work to *attempt* to differentiate what is exclusively the analyst's unconscious from what is the patient's. The case examples in the previous chapter evidence a continuous struggle in this regard.

This breaking down of countertransferences into what could be judged as "good" or "bad" ones (hence useful or non-useful), as a necessary function of the effort to work with them, is a slightly artificial distinction, however. The countertransferences in themselves are neither positive nor negative, but simply facts and ingredients of the analysis. Thus, out of the historical *enantiodromia* from countertransference as disdained to countertransference as vital has risen a distinction which is important but possibly deceptive. It is my experience, as shown in the last chapter, that most countertransferences fall somewhere in the middle of a neurotic↔useful spectrum. They are usually not either-or, but both (or "mixed"). Various Jungians, like Fordham and Jacoby, have alluded to this. Countertransference slides along the spectrum, and the goal typically is to move it to the right, so to speak: to turn the "neurotic" into the "useful." Countertransferences often start off muddled and wind up, one would hope, bringing clarity.

There may be still another way to approach complex fusion states in the countertransference/transference situation. Countertransference may not simply entail the analyst falling victim to his own prior neuroses *or* introjecting his patient's projected parts in syntonic or complementary ways. The polarity can be looked at in a more complicated manner, such that both ends of the neurotic↔useful spectrum are simultaneously in play. From this viewpoint, one requires the other.

For example, an analyst, following classical Freud rather than the more spontaneous Jung, may be by technique and conscious style a "blank screen." However, he is unconsciously never that[5], regardless of his own persona or the efficacy of his training (or self-) analysis. In fact the opposite could be argued – namely that the better the (training) analysis the greater the breadth and depth of emotional responsiveness[6] as well as understanding of oneself. This is well put by Searles when discussing analytic goals in general:

> One needs to come to reject, for example, the goal of enduring freedom from envy, or guilt, or whatnot . . . . One does not become free from feelings in the course of maturation or in the course of becoming well during psychoanalysis; one becomes, instead, increasingly free to experience feelings of all sorts.
>
> (Searles, 1966, p. 35)

This is not to suggest that the analyst's more pathological or volatile complexes should not be tamed and worked through. It is to say, though, that they are never totally worked through, and can sometimes be reconstellated under the impact of the patient's unconscious. In addition, it is possible (and even likely within a Jungian theoretical framework) that the never or "not yet" conscious may emerge from the unconscious matrix at any time. Thus Jung speaks of "pioneer work" in working with the transference (1946, p. 178) and clearly states in a later work that:

> No analysis is capable of banishing all unconsciousness forever. The analyst must go on learning endlessly, and never forget that each new case brings new problems to light and thus gives rise to *unconscious assumptions that have never before been constellated.*
>
> (Jung, 1951a, p. 116, italics mine)

Countertransference-based work, at least the variety that involves "mutual transformation," rests a great deal on this kind of attitude. To continue the point above, it is not only where the patient feels troubled but where the analyst also does that transformation takes place. As the cases attempted to show, something of parallel depth and sometimes parallel confusion goes on in the analyst. Therefore, for the analyst in countertransference the source of the transformation is not just *to use* his well-analyzed self-knowledge but to really *get "used"* by the client. This seems to involve something more than empathy based on a transient identification, however deep that is. The analyst must in a certain way feel that he has or at least shares a problem.

This "problem" may be less a "neurotic countertransference" than what has been termed a "countertransference neurosis," to reverse the emphasis and borrow Racker's phrase (1953, p. 107). Tower also speculates that:

> in many – perhaps every – intensive analytic treatment there develops something in the nature of *countertransference structures* (perhaps even a "neurosis") which are essential and inevitable counterparts of the transference neurosis . . . . I believe they function in the manner of a catalytic agent in the treatment process.
>
> (Tower, 1956, p. 232, italics mine)

In Jungian terms this falls under the rubric of "wounded-healer" phenomena. There is a new, tangible version of the patient's problem in the analyst, which is based in some way on a new constellation (or re-constellation) of the analyst's problems. Seen in this light, the "neurotic vs. useful" distinction mentioned above becomes something like this: for this particular style of countertransference work to be useful, it first has to be personal. Pushing this reversal of the situation still further, one might say that the more "personalized" the countertransference can become, the greater the potential utility and healing. Or, in Jungian terms: for "wounded healer" work to be healing, the analyst has to be really wounded by the patient, the deeper the better.

Parenthetically, the word "wounded" is preferable to "neurotic," as the latter implies a more unconscious state. "Neurosis," recently dropped from formal psychiatric nomenclature, is not an easily definable word and tends to be pejorative. Tower's above suggestion of corresponding "countertransference structures" is more accurate. L. Harvey refers more precisely to "the inevitable residues of one's own wounds" (personal communication, 1990). Perhaps the idea of a progression could again be enlisted, such that the movement from an unaware condition to a more consciously wounded state is what is most desirable. This is a fundamentally different understanding of countertransference than its being either "neurotic" or "useful." It is in between but underlying the two ends of the spectrum – a state of sometimes rather acute "analyst vulnerability." Countertransference, then, has to do with the analyst's capacity to be wounded.

The projection "hook"/the analyst's "wounds"

Further elucidation of this type of countertransference orientation requires exploration of this state of analyst vulnerability. It seems appropriate to focus on the nature and usage of projection "hooks," that is, on the very wounds onto or into which patients project (often incisively). While the analyst may experience such projections as disturbing or aggressive, it seems to be an unconscious process on the part of the patient. In terms of this discussion, projective identification is not simply a defensive/hostile move by patients to rid themselves of objectionable feelings, though that is a reasonable view. My sense of it is more Jungian (or perhaps more Kohutian) than Kleinian, so to speak – there is a positive purpose involved. From this perspective the patient must find or possibly even create areas of parallel "woundedness" in the analyst. The patient, to repeat, does this without knowing it. It is as if the unconscious wanted to bring the patient's wounds directly into the analytic situation, or induce an empathic reality almost beyond "vicarious introspection" (Kohut) and entirely in the therapeutic "here and now."

To put it another way, this seems to be a process that is a step "beyond empathy." Aside from their shift in focus (from patient to analyst), countertransference wounds often seem different than empathy in terms of feeling tone, specificity and depth. A countertransference wound may provide the basis for empathy, but the usual empathic state seems more transient and less "hooked." Empathy typically is more easy-going, perhaps more like a syntonic than the more abrasive complementary counter-transference (see Lambert, 1972). While introjective identification with the patient in this way might be some sort of "ultimate empathy," there does appear to be a fundamental difference in degree and quality between a "countertransference wound" and empathy as usually described.

This aside, due to the complicating nature of unconscious interactions there has been an inclination to view projections, as noted above, as "yours" or "mine." This back-and-forth model, worthy as it is, does not quite speak to the phenomenology of many countertransference states. The cases described in Chapter 3 reveal many instances where the patient projects something onto/into the therapist, who is then *unsure* whether the attri-butions are correct or not. In Jung's terms (1951a, p. 116), the patient may have "scored" off the therapist. Unless he assumes that the patient is necessarily wrong or projectively identifying, the therapist is forced to at least consider what the patient is suggesting. Heretofore, such self-scrutiny has sometimes been justified in Jungian circles in the course of "objectively" inter-preting a transference or countertransference dream. Now, even without dreams as pointers, the analyst may find himself looking directly at some wound into which patients project. Depending on the analyst's attitude toward that psychological vulnerability – how detached, sympathetic, dubious, anxious, etc. – he will so respond internally to the patient's idea. As noted in the last chapter's cases, there are moments when a therapist can "ground" the transference projections by privately acknowledging, how-ever reluctantly, the ways in which they could be accurate.

Attitudes toward the factual bases in the analyst's psyche for the patient's projections have varied interestingly over the years. Jung writes in Volume 6 of his *Collected Works*:

> The image we form of a human object is, to a very large extent, subjectively conditioned. In practical psychology, therefore, we would do well to make a rigorous distinction between the image or *imago* of a man and his real existence.
>
> (Jung, 1921a, p. 473)

This "subjective" approach, Jung's hallmark and a great contribution to psychology (making it "psychological" rather than "objective"), is further amplified later. Citing a case example, Jung says:

> Up till now everybody has been convinced that the idea "my father," "my mother," etc., is nothing but a factual reflection of the real parent . . . . X's idea of the father is a complex quality for which the real father is only in part responsible, an indefinitely larger share falling to the son.
>
> (Jung, 1951b, p. 18)

These statements apply equally to the transference, which Jung considers a "specific form" of projection (1935a, p. 136).

For all this subjective emphasis, however, Jung also suggestively states in "The Psychology of the Transference":

> Experience shows that the carrier of the projection is not just *any* object but is always one that proves adequate to the nature of the content projected – that is to say, it must offer the content a "hook" to hang on.
>
> (Jung, 1946, p. 291)

It is notable too that the example Jung frequently uses to exemplify the compensatory nature of dreams is his own treatment-corrective countertransference dream (Jung, 1937, p. 333), which he interprets primarily in an "objective" fashion.

Basically Jung left it there, though he did, despite his preference for archetypal-symbolic discussions, suggest the existence of down-to-earth, mutually affective analytic states – upon which the analyst's "hooks" would tacitly have bearing. Most of the countertransference writers cited in this book's literature review (particularly Blomeyer, Groesbeck and Schwartz-Salant) are pushing and expanding this concept, at least by implication. One could easily infer also that Goodheart would call the analyst's "hooks" parts of the analyst's "shadow" (to use another Jungian term).

The value, among others, of Goodheart's "listening" method is that it alerts the analyst to the existence of these constellated shadow components or "hooks." Other equally important signals include: direct or indirect imagery of the analyst in dreams or fantasy (analyst's or patient's), direct statements by the client, likely possibilities based on the analyst's prior self-knowledge, and, often underlying the above, an in-session sense of discomfort or resistance in the analyst.

Alerted by whatever means to his internal processes, what the analyst then does with his wounds is important. His "hooks" form the basis for countertransference-oriented work. They are the kernel or seed from which the transference grows. Thus, when a patient (or his imagery) says something like "You are rigid and heartless like my father," my experience is to believe him. The cases demonstrate this style of receiving projections repeatedly. This *is* what can be called "introjective identification"; however, the important component of it is that specific hooks are then engaged. Thus, experientially, it is not an "as if" phenomenon (unless all analysis is). Nor is it as temporary or transient as might be preferred. In other words, in terms of the analytic situation, *I am what they say I am*. Theoretically speaking, this would be a variation on Plaut's (1956) "incarnation" theme, combined with elements of Goodheart's method.

The analyst's internal response to this predicament ideally might not be defensive but receptive: not "No way!" but "Hmm, is that so?" The analyst receives it in this fashion – "voluntarily and consciously taking over the psychic sufferings of the patient" (Jung, 1946, p. 176) – and only *then* begins to work on it. From this perspective, he works on it because he has to. From the patient's perspective, the patient must "find" this hook, however unconsciously he does this, in the analyst. The analyst probably has enough shadow components, somewhere, to form the basis of the hook. In the event that the patient cannot find one, and hence does not affect or constellate the analyst, then the analyst might search for one (or check his resistance). Failing that, this style of countertransference-based analysis will not run as deep as it could have, or perhaps even fail.

A central point here is that the patient's unconscious contents can be nourished rather than restricted by the analyst's "wounds."

Depending on one's attitude to the word, one can call the patient's wounds "pathological." If so, following the idea of shadow and hooks promoted here, one can then say that the patient's pathology constellates the analyst's. Accordingly, analysts need not try to eliminate their pathology, but know it and utilize it. This does not mean enacting it, but does mean a fluid awareness of new and old shadow as well as a concern not to rationalize or project this upon the client. Searles addresses this mutuality of shadow as honestly as anyone, and cautions analysts against "using the patient to bear the burden of all the severe psychopathology in the whole relationship" (Searles, 1978, pp. 62–63). From a Jungian perspective a "wounded healer" does not mean a "once wounded – now recovered" one, but one who is currently *vulnerable* as well (the Latin word "vulnus" means "wound").

Transformational aspects

Because the analyst's identification with the patient is based on real components of his (the analyst's) own personality, and because he and the patient are thereby locked in mutual woundedness, it follows that the work the analyst does on himself can have direct effect on the patient's complexes. The process begins with the analyst's admission, so to speak, that the patient's attributions are in some way correct. Whether this ultimately proves to be true is not of primary importance. The main thing is that the analyst now experiences the reality component of their conjoined complexes. He does this by listening for and exploring what Searles aptly calls the "nuclei of reality" (1975b, p. 374) – the hooks – that form the basis of the client's projections.

This blurring of the patient/analyst boundary could be called a regressive one, a kind of regression in service of the healing. To the therapist it feels like a regression on his own behalf, though he also knows it is "for" the patient and treatment. As the analyst slowly integrates the client's inner realities, which are grounded now in the analyst's own, the client slowly synthesizes too. The image they share of a "patient," and that both participate in psychologically, is gradually repaired. A good portion of this work is the analyst's, depending on the patient's development; or at least the nature of their respective contributions to the task may be different. In fact, the analyst's level of stress may vary in proportion to the patient's levels of defense and consciousness.

That is, the more disturbed or unintegrated the patient's self, the more the analyst gets the patient's unconscious "head-on," so to speak. The unconscious material is either more or less "unfiltered" or "unimpeded," depending on the client's ego-defenses (A. Hill, personal communication, 1991). To the extent that the patient's unconscious is unhindered, the analyst absorbs it directly. The analyst's "work" level varies accordingly.

It should be emphasized again that these are subtle feeling processes, more experiential than interpretive. For the patient it is as if his unconscious projections are really "seen" in the reality of the analyst. The purpose of interpretation may be less to give back information or insight per se, though this can be important at a different level (ego, consciousness, "adult"). Rather, interpretation clarifies for himself and subtly communicates to the client the analyst's empathy and participation in the mutual process. But incarnation is more crucial for the client than interpretation as such. Dieckmann's (1974) ideas about the secondary nature of interpretation are relevant here, as are Schwartz-Salant's (1989, p. 109) on "sacrificing" interpretations. The patient's perspective, essentially non-interpretive, and the therapeutic action are well described by Searles:

> The patient comes to see in the therapist all the figures of his own past, and these percepts have become now so free from anxiety that the patient can (partly by identification with the therapist who can accept within himself the reality nuclei for his being so perceived) discover them in himself, too, with a freedom which enables him to now experience them as really acceptable components of his own self.
>
> (Searles, 1976, p. 532)

Over a period of time, it may be said that the analyst "takes in" more than the past conflicts or components of the patient. It is in a Jungian sense the other's whole Self, and the conscious and unconscious "feeling-image" thereof, that the analyst carries. The analyst is "holding," helping to create this image of the patient as treatment proceeds, much as a parent absorbs, bonds with and nourishes a child, literally and imaginatively. The mother's musings during (and after) pregnancy might be an accurate metaphor[7], except the analyst does not start from scratch. As in actual parenting, there are complex dynamics around needs, images, power, incest, ambitions, demands, etc. To describe it this

113

way is not necessarily to infantilize the patient. All this is a process of feeling and imagination, perhaps something like an extended active imagination about the patient (see Davidson, 1966).

After a while, the analyst may see the child in the patient. More precisely it is the "inner child," the *potential* self, of the patient that is thus held and promoted. The analyst's seemingly rather naive, undefended absorption of the patient in itself has an unboundaried, childish quality; hence, it brings into play the analyst's own "inner child" in its similar woundedness, hopefulness, or whatever. Therefore it is safe to suggest that the aforementioned "inner patient" in both participants in this process is well characterized as an "inner child." This is consistent with the many facets of the "child:" as an historical, developmental fact or as a futuristic, more eternal, Self-symbol. In other words patients come in for treatment of their "child," whether this turns out to be their childhood or their current "growth" (or both, as is usually the case).

This mention of the convergence of child-self, Self and inner patient in both participants raises another issue about "Self." Since the demand for "incarnation" is high in this form of countertransference-based work, a special premium is placed on the analyst's linkage to his own sense of Self. The "impact" (Fordham, 1979, p. 635) of the patient's unconscious, alone or in combination with the analyst's accessible "wounds," may periodically throw the analyst off center. Within this countertransference paradigm described here, it may even be necessary that the analyst be "lost" on occasion, together with the patient, so that the patient can then be "found." However, the work (and the patient) ultimately rely on the analyst's being rooted in or successfully re-establishing his relationship with the Self. The cases give evidence, in and out of session, of the difficult nature of that struggle[8].

Thus by working on himself and continually maintaining the ego–self axis, the analyst is performing therapeutic work on the patient. Proper initial safeguards are important, so that the analyst is not primarily or blindly working on strictly private issues that are not linked to the patient. Once these safeguards (which will be discussed more later) are in place, then the shared, "wounded" vectors in the countertransference and relationship become primary. Following this, the other aspect of the wounded-healer archetype moves to the fore – the "healing" side. But how does this self-therapeutic work of the analyst come to effect the patient's healing process?

On one level the analyst is always striving to sort out what is his from what is the patient's. This is a constant, which relates to Jung's "clean hands" approach and occurs both before and during analysis. The shadow must be understood and/or contained as much as possible to prevent acting out, retaliation, or even pro-longed dysfunction of the therapist. It is desirable for the analyst to contaminate the process as little as possible. This sorting out is a discriminating function, logos-oriented perhaps, which actually paves the way for the client's "infection" of the analyst. It is one half of this type of countertransference-based work.

There is another level or area in which, paradoxically, the analyst participates more fully in the projections. While on the one hand sorting out his realities from the patient's projections and vice versa, the analyst on the other hand "accepts" or incar-nates the projections. This relates to a fused, eros-oriented style of experience.

When there is a shift in the analyst at this interlocking un-conscious level, there is a parallel shift in the patient, due to their merged state. Hence, the explanation for change may be slightly different than Searles' suggestion that the patient identifies with the analyst's self-analysis and then introjects it. Though some-thing indeed happens, perhaps it is not so much a matter of "giving back" something to the patient in any direct, sequential sense. Hence the giving back of interpretations is less important, though this can depend on the patient and situation[9]. The real "giving back" has happened already via the identification-based empathy. The identity of analyst and patient is already there in the process and unconscious interchanges are therefore simul-taneous. Just as the infection by the patient takes place in a phenomenologically real way in the analyst, so the detoxification of the analyst's constellated and parallel wounds takes place on the patient's wounded levels. The mutual identification is that deep. At the same time there are levels closer to the surface, more in the realm of the "ego," where the identity lessens and divides. Visually, this might look like a "V". This style of working em-phasizes the bottom parts of the V.

In terms of "time" factors, the simultaneity of this process fits with Dieckmann's (1976) view that synchronicity is a prime explanation for the chaining of patient/analyst associations. Synchronicity, in Jungian terms, seems to relativize cause–effect, space–time coordinates and focus on a new plane mediated by meaning. In the unconscious (and when two people connect in the unconscious) communications sometimes appear to happen at the speed of light, which makes sequences imperceptible – events then seem to be virtually simultaneous. Furthermore, when in the medium of the conjoined unconscious, the source or locus of psychic events (i.e. whose dream? whose unconscious?) and their sequence in time (future–past reversals, precognition, etc.) may become scrambled. Standard paradigms of explanation become insufficient. However, this is not necessarily to postulate the ESP or parapsychological bases of the countertransference process that Dieckmann seems to (1974, p. 82). Nor is the focus of this book as much geared towards associative chains per se as towards an actual working through, quite mundane and grounded, in the analyst. Still, Dieckmann's ideas may be the best current explanation.

The analyst's pole of the wounded-healer archetype thus has much to do with the rainmaker as idea and ideal. Like the Taoist sage, the analyst gets straight with himself so the healing waters will flow, but the drought, so to speak, has been placed *in* the analyst and has reconstellated his own internal drought (or wounds). He gets in Tao (works through his simultaneous, parallel wounds), and thereby the fused patient does too. An important point here is that the rainmaker ideal is achieved, not "given," and follows a stirred-up, countertransference feeling, usually of impressive magnitude. One gets to the rainmaker position. Each transference/countertransference component that really "hooks" the analyst initiates a re-working of this process.

This countertransference process also can be looked at locally as well as more generally. That is, there are specific counter-transference pieces that may be worked with session by session – little bits of working through, empathy and so on. In the mean-time, at another level alluded to in the cases (and on p. 113), there is an overall picture or image of the patient. This is slowly re-shaping and evolving over the course of the analysis – the idea and "sense" of this particular patient is being refined in the analyst's unconscious. The fantasies (admittedly quite personal) I tend to have of this activity are of slow-moving "nature" pro-cesses at work (thus I have at times called this developmental process "organic" in this book). This may not be conscious very often. In my experience, at various points the analyst happens to notice that the "whole patient" feels different to him in some way. The patient has "become," let's say, healthy or better.

This is obviously some kind of intuitive-feeling process about the client and therefore should be examined by the therapist for its authenticity and objectivity. This seemingly improved patient-image *can* be a product of defensiveness, ambition or narcissistic need in the analyst, for example, or possibly a complementary countertransference (e.g. of a parental imago). Fortunately, this perceptual shift can be checked against external reality. The therapist merely has to watch against his own self-deception.

However, the spontaneous appearance of this change is in any case significant, especially if it has not appeared before. Patients are affected and potentially limited not only by what we can see in ourselves but what we can authentically "see" in them, or for them (see Guggenbuhl-Craig, 1971). If we cannot eventually envision their health, improvement or, better, their wholeness, then they will not envision them. This would be a failure of mirroring. Yet this vision is hard-won and moves very slowly in some cases. It is not a matter of an upbeat outlook or confidence about the analytic process. It is a psychotherapeutic creation coming out of the countertransference/transference fusion, an evolution out of the identity with the original, broken condition of the "patient."

In overall terms, the therapist is made "sick" by the patient in this type of deep healing process. The former then cures himself and thereby cures the patient. From this perspective, one could say that the phenomenology of the transference is in fact that the patient's illness is "transferred" to the doctor – a situation Jung first warns about, then suggests is an occupational hazard of analysis (Jung, 1946, pp. 172, 176–177). This transfer is not made onto a blank screen, the analyst being no more what Jung calls a *tabula rasa* than the patient is. Indeed it is the very "hooks" and activated complexes in the analyst that enable the transference to "ground" and then be worked through by the analyst's self (meaning the entirety of his conscious-unconscious processes).

"The patient as therapist to his analyst"

Is psychotherapy, as an old joke suggests, "When two people

who need help get it"? The analyst undoubtedly benefits from the work too, and not only because the patient enables him to fulfill his vocation, get paid for it, and explore or re-explore his inner processes. Jung notes how both participants are "altered" or "transformed" in the process (Jung, 1946, pp. 171, 199). Dieckmann (1974, p. 75) suggests that two "individuation" opportunities are presented to the analyst: one through his participation with the patient and another through his self-analysis[10]. Goodheart's original work (1980) makes considerable use of Langs' approaches and, much less so, Searles', both of which stress that the patient aids the analyst. Searles, probably our most profound and liberating writer on countertransference, makes the following comments on the mutuality of the process early on:

> The therapist, at the deepest levels of the therapeutic interaction, temporarily introjects the patient's pathogenic conflicts and deals with them at an intrapsychic, unconscious as well as conscious, level, bringing to bear upon them the capacities of his own relatively strong ego, and then, similarly by introjection, the patient benefits from this intrapsychic work which has been accomplished by the therapist. *Incidentally, I believe that the patient, on not infrequent occasions, gives the therapist the same kind of therapeutic help with the latter's intrapsychic conflicts.*
>
> (Searles, 1958, p. 214, italics mine)

Searles goes on in a 1975 work, "The Patient as Therapist to His Analyst," to insist that the patient has unmet psychotherapeutic strivings towards his parents that have to be reenacted successfully in the transference. That is, his cure involves his having "been *in reality* at least partially successful as a therapist who has been attempting to help the analyst" (Searles, 1975a, p. 384). In Jungian "wounded healer" terms, this would mean the establishment of an effective "inner healer" by means of a cure of the analyst's wounds. Thus the analyst's introjective healing of the patient is reciprocated by the patient towards the analyst. This clearly goes further than Langs' "bipersonal field" ideas – Searles is not talking about transference displacements or cues, but about actual cures.

Searles' ideas naturally create narcissistic and philosophical resistances, as he is talking about something more personal than "learning" from the patient. Perhaps the difficulty is that his ideas threaten one's professional sense that the burden of the analytic "help" should fall on the analyst himself. While Searles may not be suggesting otherwise, his hypothesis does raise the question of who is curing whom (and who pays). It is a radical vision – as Searles says, "nothing less than a metamorphosis in our concepts of the nature of the curative process" (1975a, p. 384) – and one that can obviously be abused by the therapist's "charlatan" shadow. It walks a dangerous line, and depends on the therapist's near-total integrity; but then, so does all countertransference-based work.

In Searles' paradigm, the analyst will be relying upon the "therapist" that is in the patient to introject and in effect treat the "patient" that is in him (the analyst). However, I am less inclined to think the patient cures the analyst, though he might unconsciously sense how much pathology the analyst has or where the analyst really "is," psychologically. The patient's unconscious is often correct as to what is real. No less is the analyst's unconscious perceptive. Many patients do have accurate "radar" (see Miller, 1981), yet this does not mean they are analysts. While we do take conscious and unconscious cues from the patient (to the point of embodying his projections or listening à la Goodheart), a continuous effort must be made *not* to burden him. Again, Searles is not saying that analysts should burden patients; rather, perhaps, that they cannot avoid it. Patients will introject therapists regardless. As Jung says, "The patient *reads* the personality of the analyst . . . for nothing is finer than the empathy of a neurotic" (Jung, 1914, p. 277). Still, the analyst's containment of the experientially real pathology and his working it through in a more or less private way is closer to the appropriate source of healing.

The ultimate responsibility for countertransference must rest with the analyst. Among other things, the patient may identify with that unceasing *effort*. In the same early, clinical correspondence cited above (in which he also first stressed that the analyst's "personality is one of the main factors in the cure"), Jung seemed to allude to something like this analytic responsibility:

> Patients read the analyst's character intuitively, and they should find in him a man with failings, admittedly, but also a man who strives at every point to fulfill his human duties in the fullest sense.
>
> (Jung, 1914, p. 260)

Therefore it might be not only the reworked content of the analyst's countertransference work that the patient introjects, but the processing and integrity itself. This places the analytic emphasis a good deal less on the patient than Searles does. *Because* the patient will inevitably introject the analyst's unconscious (just as the patient did his own parents'), the analyst has an added burden – not to be untouched (the opposite in fact), but to contain his own and his patient's material as much as possible.

A COUNTERTRANSFERENCE MODEL

The general theoretical picture sketched above provides the background for a more specific model for working with countertransference in a transformative way. What follows is a rough, "how to" paradigm.

Certain aspects of this model are applicable to any style of doing analysis, not just a countertransference-based one, so the model is not exclusive or, in spots, original[11]. It is not written in stone either: the "model" should be taken loosely, and is therefore presented anecdotally. This outline is a distillation of highly individualized processes that may occur in (and out of) a single session or a lengthy series of sessions (i.e. a whole analysis). However, there are no "typical" sessions or analyses, really, though over time one can recognize some familiar ground.

What is presented as a *sequence* of events here is actually a group of events that overlap each other considerably. Elements of each segment may exist in the others, and what may seem like distinct activities are sometimes part and parcel of the same, almost instantaneous process. On the other hand, long periods of time may be spent struggling in one of the stages. Time elements therefore may not be equal in different parts of this skeletal model. Nor is it a "one-time" paradigm: it is best to say one continuously re-cycles through it. This process may speed up with repetition; that is, one can frequently pick up where one left off the last time with the patient. Old ground need not always be re-traced. Also, some aspects of countertransference seem to get left for awhile, then returned to later.

Thus, it is difficult to set up a precise model of these countertransference processes because they are relatively unfixed. Sequential, simultaneous and unevenly balanced operations are in effect. There is also, visually speaking, what seems to be a vertical dimension: there are multiple constellations "in the air" most of the time, like airplanes circling an airport at different altitudes before landing. One or several may predominate for a given time. In addition, resistance can be a central feature of the analyst's experience at any point.

This process entails a large number of small, half-conscious decisions by the analyst (and probably by the patient). Only a few of the more major decision points will be described here.

Preliminary

The first stage in this model could simply be called the *preliminary* one. This occurs before there has been any contact at all with the patient. It involves preparations on both a large and small scale for doing work with a countertransference focus. Its core, naturally, has to do with the therapist's self-knowledge, personal development and basic attitudes. Contributing factors are, first and foremost, the training analysis, followed (in no particular order) by the analyst's training in general, clinical experience, supervision and previous experience with countertransference struggles. It helps, no doubt, to have been through these wars before. It also helps to have something of the fateful attitude Jung describes so well:

> The doctor knows – or at least he should know – that he did not choose his career by chance; and the psychotherapist in particular should clearly understand that psychic infections, however superfluous they seem to him, are in fact the predestined concomitants of his work, and thus fully in accord with the instinctive disposition of his own life.
>
> (Jung, 1946, p. 177)

But whatever the therapist feels about his motivations for doing analysis, he, specifically in this preparatory stage, must be "ready to roll." The first contacts with patients strongly color countertransference (as the examples in Chapter 3 show). An anxious client meets a not necessarily less anxious analyst. The "projectiles," as Plaut (1956, p. 156) says, may be flying. The analyst, while not necessarily being defensive, wants to "hit the ground running;" that is, be in his analytic mode or analytic identity from the outset[12].

121

Clearing the field

The second stage of countertransference work might be called *clearing the field*. This applies, of course, to the very first session, but also to subsequent ones. The point is to create a state of openness both to the patient's unconscious and to one's own unconscious in relation to that particular patient. Though this does not require a special technique, it does involve concentrating one's consciousness (and unconscious) on the patient, perhaps a sort of centering or meditative-reflective state. When Jung said, "Learn your theories as well as you can, but put them aside" (1973a, p. 84), or when Bion speaks of beginning sessions without "memory" of past sessions and without "desires for results, 'cure' or even understanding" (quoted in Langs, 1990, p. 244), they are referring to this state of mind. Freud's "evenly hovering attention" (1912, p. 118) may express it with regard to more relaxed moments in analysis. The goal at any rate is to see what may arise freshly from the interaction.

Despite the above admonitions, it may also be practical to review notes on the previous session before the new one begins. This can help re-orient the therapist toward what is happening with the patient – a sort of "warm-up" period. Having re-contacted him in this way, then the content itself can be put aside, if one prefers. In addition, it may be useful to reflect on the patient in no specific way, to see what one feels about him, what is coming up in the countertransference. Note-taking or writing can assist with this. Also, both to provide emotional closure at the end of the session and to clear the field for the next client, brief countertransference notes can be written immediately after the hour[13]. Again, all these efforts, which are personalized and time-consuming, are primarily to warm up the therapist's empathy towards that special patient. Analysis, at least some of the time, is a creative process too, and such rituals can also help concentrate energies for that.

These between-session activities can have more than just pre-paratory value as well. I once made the mistake of calling up a doctor between patients to get some test results (on me). Not unexpectedly, the doctor told me that I indeed did have an easily treatable skin "*CANCER*" in my left armpit. Alarmed, my feelings pinballed from realism to upset to denial and back around again with a speed that was quite fascinating (in retrospect). Equally interesting was when my next patient revealed that her husband had stomach cancer. My emotional upset fortunately helped form the preparatory basis for deeper empathic understanding in this difficult hour.

The case examples naturally show considerable use of self-analytic reflection activities on a larger scale, not just immediately before and after sessions. The more difficult the situation, the more work involved. In this kind of countertransference work the therapist often carries his patients around with him, consciously or unconsciously. What Jung lyrically says about dreams is relevant or even inevitable for countertransference: "Look at it from all sides, take it in your hand, carry it about with you, let your imagination play round it" (Jung, 1933, p. 320). Much of this is non-session activity and, when "hooked," much of it is unavoidable.

Reception

Having got up to speed, the next discernible stage of the proto-type is the internal *reception* of the patient by the analyst. This is a complex operation, consisting of multiple attention processes, in which the analyst's attention is directed both outwards, empathically, toward the client and inwards toward himself. Throughout the entire analysis the analyst will be alternately imagining, "seeing" or feeling from the patient's perspective (empathy) and then from his own (countertransference).

Specifically, having cleared the field, the analyst "takes in" the client and then may react in ways he begins to notice. Essentially he attends to his thoughts, fantasies and emotional states. Literally anything can come up; it may be desirable to associate more or less within the context of the patient's statements or material (roughly similar to Jung's recommendations about staying with the dream images themselves). But a freer, less "Jungian" association process seems perfectly valid too.

There is a vast range of stimuli the analyst can react to, the primary one being the patient's content and style of presentation. Then, in this growing web of associations, there are the analyst's own reactions, which in turn may spin further fantasies. More sensate stimuli are also available. For example, facial resemblances, clothes, or word use may remind the analyst, vaguely and half-consciously, of someone he knows. Recognizing the resemblance permits the therapist to notice how the feeling tone of the therapeutic relationship has been colored. Further meanings or hypotheses may then follow, as the therapist reflects on the possible relevance to the patient of this connection (or the relevance of his patient's resembling a friend, let's say). Perhaps in a similar, intuitive fashion, moods of patients in the waiting room sometimes seem immediately, and accurately, detectable. Being open to the patient, the patient registers.

Selection

Out of this vast array of inputs a *selection* process begins. Mainly it is the patient who unconsciously selects the material to be focussed on. The analyst may see or hear things that especially interest him, for whatever reasons. However, because the patient can be so readily influenced by the analyst's choices, it would seem important simply to let the patient's unconscious unfold and lead the way. The analyst is steered in his countertransference by his silent responses to the patient's material – unless the analyst finds himself preoccupied or distracted. Sometimes the client will jump to another topic, leaving the analyst trailing along the previous one in his countertransference. Here the analyst may have to hustle to get back on the track, and here one finds numerous therapist interventions, made in order to punctuate the shift or slow things down. Many therapist comments, often of the empathic variety, are merely markers on the trail, or pauses so the therapist can swallow. Other comments, particularly ones that are interpretive or confrontative, affect this selection process profoundly and mark the *analyst's* contribution to it. This is why the analyst must listen carefully to the next responses to any intervention. Ultimately, the patient's selection of material is governed by both participants' associative processes.

Containment

The chief feature of the next phase is *containment*. In an individual session and over many sessions, as the patient focusses, the analyst does. There is a narrowing or deepening which seems to naturally evolve. Deeper emotional areas yield deeper countertransference responses, as do direct patient statements, fantasies or dreams about the analyst. Also, countertransference dreams and/or non-session work may produce a certain readiness to descend, as it were, with the client. And the analyst may have been listening for indirect sources for transference reference: dreams, talk about others, and history might all be "imagined" as possibly having such reference. Typically, there is some recognizable experience of greater anxiety in the analyst, emanating from any of the above sources. Something unconscious begins to "take," in the countertransference, which is characterized by the analyst's rise in tension (or perhaps expectancy).

This state does not of course have to occur "later" in the work. There are patients who by attack or other means push into the therapist immediately (see p. 131). They do not politely or gradually move into a deeper place where the analyst may follow; instead they provoke intense, unconscious feeling states. Regardless of source or timing, the main feature of this deepening, experiential phase is the analyst's containment of the unconscious. Here is where he has to "hold," under pressure, and not resort to various actings out to relieve the tension.

Working through

When the anxiety flags go up, the analyst's focus turns ever more inward to contain and struggle with it. This can be brief, but in deeper instances it may be a long-term process. It is important here to amplify, elucidate, give rein to fantasy and feeling, all in service of the question: how *am* I reacting to this? Part of this *working through* stage involves resistance in the analyst – because accepting induction of conflicted or anxiety-producing states is painful. Thus there are repeated struggles with what might be termed "introjective resistance." Narcissistic or superego resistance would not be unusual either.

As one moves through resistant states, many questions can then be asked: is it true, what this patient says about me? If so, how so? Or, how might it be true? What sort of wounds or difficulties does this patient raise in me? Having pursued some of these, the focus often tends to switch back to the patient: "Is it him or is it me?" Thus the problem begins to be pushed back toward the patient. The analyst is here sorting out his "neurotic" countertransferences from what could be the neurotic transference projections.

Further back and forth along these lines may result in the

analyst drawing a conclusion like "The patient is putting this into me." Accordingly, he may hypothesize about the shape of that particular imago in the client's unconscious. Conclusions may form about what all this is saying, primarily about the patient and his unconscious, but also about the analyst, analytic interaction, historical antecedents, prospective possibilities, parallels in other relationships and in the analytic one, etc.

If, or as, these things become relatively clarified in this "working through" phase, the therapist is at another decision point; namely, whether to tell the patient what he "sees." If he decides to interpret out loud, there are very subtle choices of emphasis involved. These are mostly determined by the patient's ego and emotional states and the particular context of the session, but there are multiple factors from previous work and history also to be considered.

Particularly if a clearer interpretive vision of the situation has not hatched yet, or sometimes even if it has, the analyst may continue with his "containment" policy. When one sees something, it can be difficult not to say so, especially if it relieves internal pressure. The therapist may want to consider whether it is primarily his tension that he wants to relieve. Another option is to "sacrifice" the outer expression of the interpretation. This is not to suggest sacrificing the understandings, nor to suggest that, even unsaid, interpretations may not still have silent "effect" (registered somehow in the patient through intuition, resonances mediated via the Self, body language shifts detected in the analyst[14], etc.). But the main thrust of the analyst's integrative activity can be also toward his own wound, which is shared with the patient unconsciously, rather than toward the patient's separate one.

Incubation

Thus, instead of interpreting back to the patient, an analyst may choose or be forced to *incubate* the anxiety-ridden states and work them through further in himself. The analyst here is incarnating, in a submerged or suspended state. He is purposely and purposefully letting the contamination deepen. In and out of session he continues to work through, still following the path of his own "hooks." He struggles, monitors and ponders, using notes, dreams and fantasies. Overall the analyst has here done a kind of "double dip," voluntarily or sometimes involuntarily electing to go down again. It is also useful to remember that the "interpreting vs. incubating" is not entirely clear-cut. It seems the analyst actually does both within his countertransference experience.

Along the way different "feeling-images" of the patient may occur, which the therapist can also monitor. These overall pictures are countertransference measures of the patient's situation. This is a less immediate plane of countertransference experience. They tend to come as a discovery. Like shifts in dream imagery over time, they may be registers of the unconscious. But they need to be watched. So when these spontaneous images of the patient do arise, the question then is: have I changed or has the client?

Validation

Therefore, regardless of which fork the analyst has tended to accent – incubation or interpretation – some general *validation* procedures are necessary. When the analyst has been struggling faithfully with countertransference issues, a "felt" shift in the overall image (or in the quality, tone or anxiety level in the session) can be perceived. An accompanying, relieving sense of understanding and insight may contribute to the so-called "'aha!' experience." In general, and with suitable conscientiousness on the analyst's part, these imaginal changes in the "patient" can be trusted as accurate indications of shifts (or potentialities) in the actual patient. The client's associations, à la Langs, can also be either an effective monitor of change or a response to specific interventions based on these countertransference processes, silent or spoken. More generally, indications of "movement" or lack thereof in the patient can be perceived by the honestly objective observer-analyst. Furthermore, direct patient statements help gauge psychic changes, as do overt behavioral changes (keeping in mind compliance tendencies, the patient's degree of observing ego, and the state of the working alliance). Unconscious products, especially dreams in patient or analyst, may confirm shifts in the analytic situation and the patient's inner life. A deepening of the personality, more accessible feelings, more intimate relationships, more consciousness – all these contribute to a validation of the countertransference image evolving in the analyst, too.

The analyst's best safeguard, though, against countertransference error is a continual consideration of the question, "Is it him or is it me?" This is a taxing question that cannot always be answered with certainty. Thus the constant attention to it is a proper preventative against its abuse or inaccuracy. It does not hurt for the therapist to err on the side of considering it his own problem. To do so is no more than what he asks patients to do in their relationships – take care of their own end of it. And to do so even if wrong, is to do what patients sometimes need us to do, at least according to this model.

The countertransference-based program outlined here is also best considered as a process. Not only is the sequence somewhat arbitrary as well as continuous and oversimplified, it is also the case that the analyst may have less "say" in this process than he'd like to think. He does not direct it, he responds to aspects of it[15]. One hopes that a healing process, or the Self, or the unconscious, or whatever, is in control. This seems to be the situation, but it is often apparent only in successful cases in retrospect.

FURTHER THOUGHTS ON SOME ISSUES IN COUNTERTRANSFERENCE

The above model is oriented toward a specific brand of mutually transformative, countertransference-based interaction. We turn now to discussion of some controversial issues which come up vis-a-vis not only that model but countertransference in general. Many of the points here are arguable, just as the theory and style outlined here are. They are offered with the sure knowledge that, in a sense, everybody has a countertransference to the topic of countertransference.

The theory elucidated in this study is woven out of threads of other writers in combination with my own. That is the case as well with *their* theories. One takes in a theory and processes it in one's own way, not unlike "taking on" a patient in fact. To take in Jung's approach, for example, one perhaps experiences a certain resonance, ingests and then digests his work – according to one's own predisposition (for want of a better word) or needs. What one integrates of a theory is that theory met by that individual's "personal equation." Someone mentioned that, when learning a theory, we "re-invent" it. This is part of the picture. The other part is that one recombines theories according to one's personal taste, also adding new ingredients.

An attempt has been made here to understand unconscious

countertransference processes that will nevertheless remain mysterious. The precise nature of the unconscious in and of itself is, as the name says, "unknown." As Jung said, "the unconscious is something which is really unconscious!" (in Evans, 1976, p. 56). Various writers employ different metaphors to attempt to explain the unknowns of countertransference. Their preferences, and antecedents, are clear: Jung with alchemy, Fordham with the Kleinian model of projective identification, Dieckmann with the "Rainmaker" parable, Schwartz-Salant's "subtle body," etc. There are many countertransference keys to play in and different Jungians tend to hammer harder on different notes, again according to personal preference. My experiences and thoughts on the subject are no exception.

With countertransference, as with anything else, it is important to have metaphoric structures within which to try to grasp the phenomena. Yet there is a paradox: while it is necessary to find or create the metaphor that individually fits, it is also correct not to be too glued to one's metaphor. One's point of view may not comprehend everything (or sometimes anything) on a given day with a given client. So one should not be too wedded to one's creation. My position is individual yet "pluralistic," to use Samuels' term; it seems true, as Jung (1973b, p. 405) noted about some of his disagreements with Freud, that the same psychological "facts" can be interpreted differently. Not *all* interpretations are correct, but a valid, "good faith" case can frequently be made for more than one of them. I personally find several standpoints on countertransference to be not only tenable but meaningful and true. Therefore, one needs to find one's own viewpoint and hold to it, while not necessarily rejecting a relationship with other options.

Finally, it should be further noted that there are not only different metaphors but many different *ways* of doing countertransference-based work. As mentioned earlier (p. 105), this book's particular "vision" focuses on a hybrid of wounded-healer and rainmaker positions. This taxing, personally involved way of working is not necessarily for all therapists nor, for that matter, for all patients. Individual requirements vary from case to case.

The subject/object boundary

The above-mentioned pluralistic approach holds true especially around what could be called the boundaries of subjective/objective reality. In terms of countertransference this is an area of acute difficulty. It is not possible to say ahead of time (or perhaps ever) whether, for example, a patient's dream-image or projection onto the analyst is "true" per se. The question frequently cannot be answered *now*. Meanwhile, the analyst considers it, doubts it, "believes" it, incarnates it or does what he will with it. This book describes a process where, true or not, the analyst finds or makes it true for himself, and then uses that countertransference as a basis for the work. Countertransferences are generally true in some way, or in some part. Although the usual tendency is to separate from them, projections can also be "joined" in a sense, therapeutically.

To put the subject/object question another way: it may not be something the analyst's ego has to fight about too much. The patient and his unconscious will use the analyst as the patient sees fit. The analyst has to cooperate. For essentially healing reasons, not just defensive ones, the patient may be seen as forming his projections around, or drawing out, the analyst's new or old complexes. So, for example, if the patient (as in case two, Ms. J) dreams that a "doctor" wants to kill her, the analyst may follow a five-step sequential path that sees this as:

1 *Subjective* (a simple projection of the patient's)
2 *Projective Identification* (the therapist notes some alien, subjective feeling states in session)
3 *Projective Identification/Introjective Identification* (caught up in it, muddled, whose problem is this?)
4 *Projective Identification + "Hooks"* (finding the basis for the introjective identification, and thereby deepening it)
5 *Objective* (subjectively true in some way in the analyst)

As long as a basically conscientious analyst is conscious of it, arriving at point 5 *can* be an achievement rather than a failure. In Jung's words he has been called on to "participate" (1951a, p. 116), in the "here and now" analytic situation. In my words, he is *in* the patient's unconscious, and vice versa. According to this scheme, it is likely that his successful working through of the "objective" state reverses the sequence, goes back up the ladder, and returns the detoxified complex to the patient. Of course, it is possible too to see the above grid not as fluid process but as a static representation of five separate interpretive alternatives.

Dreams about the analyst, being right on the subject/object

divide, present many potential reference points. They may relate to the dreamer solely, to the outer world, to inner feelings about the outer world, to the analyst or to the analytic process. If not directly related to the countertransference, they may still suggest what *might* become operative or constellated there. That is, these dream figures or imagos are the complexes the analyst is likely to feel or have to embody. It is at least fair to say that the dream of the analyst strongly suggests that patient's issues are "in" the analytic process and in the room. Probably, they are in the analyst now – he will be feeling the things characterized in the image. Moreover, he (his hooks) may be contributing to the things that are characterized in the image. Alternatively, as Groesbeck seems to say, these images may be commentaries on the state of the patient's "inner healer." But it would be difficult to imagine that particular imago not being closely connected to the patient's relationship with his actual, outer healer. The analyst will be implicated in some way.

Interestingly, there is a tendency to take patient's dreams as subjective and analyst's dreams (about the patient) as objective. This again shows a certain relationship to the subject/object boundary. It may not be inappropriate, from the standpoints of the analyst's putting his unconscious at the patient's service or his having a relatively better relationship (probably) to himself. Like any other countertransference phenomenon it is mixed.

Example

Before our first session, my first analytic "control" patient told me she had spent several years on the couch with a psychoanalyst and had previously consulted a veteran Jungian analyst. She also said she "needed to get angry at a man." I was apprehensive, while naturally wanting this first case under supervision to go well.

As might be expected, this patient berated me throughout our first session in every conceivable way: I was an analyst-in-training, my office was too small and in a suite of offices, the chairs were uncomfortable, I was not the veteran Jungian analyst, I was in my head and a "thinking" type; too "Waspy," not "warm" and "Jewish;" an idiot ("Haven't you read Jung and Von Franz?!") and a failure ("Do you have *any* patients?"). She also informed me at one point, "You're going to miss your chance" (to which I drily asked, "You mean my chance to have the opportunity to work with you?").

Nevertheless, after she left I found I liked this client, and was personally pleased I had not folded or retaliated (except for the veiled sarcasm). Pondering this, I realized she bore a resemblance to an attractive friend and former colleague of mine. That night I had the first dream of the analysis: *this patient was waving her hand in front of my genital area (I was dressed) from slightly below, perhaps as if she were kneeling. She seemed curious, not grasping, as if warming her hand.*

After considerable thought, I wound up taking an "objective" and "analytic situation" approach to this dream. That is, I felt that behind her abusiveness lay a need to connect with *her* own masculine and positive animus functions (currently in the off-putting form I'd experienced that day). An idealization was involved (and consciously resisted). In terms of the analysis itself, the dream seemed to compensate the combative quality of the initial session and kept me in the game by suggesting that something different might also be going on. For me personally, it showed my beleagured "phallus" and self as superior and more interesting than this possibly envious patient would have had me believe. I imagined too, following Searles (1975a), that this analysis, my first, would require and help me to develop further my own masculine components (as indeed it already had).

But in fact this was my dream, a countertransference dream. This caused me to wonder not only about her penis envy but about a need in me for "phallic worship," related to a "castrating" aspect of my own psyche which, I hoped, might now be emerging in a more positive way and with which my work with this patient might somehow be implicated[16].

So, whose dream was this? Mine, ostensibly; about her, ostensibly. R.D. Laing suggests that a pregnant mother might be able to dream the dream of an embryo or fetus (1976). Jung analyzed a patient's "erotic and religious problem" through the dreams of his young son (Jung, 1928, p. 53). The unconscious may overarch, underlie, surround, umbilically connect or "hold" a patient and analyst like a mother holding a child.

The point of all this is that I, as therapist, chose to interpret my dream primarily as her dream (or the dream of *our* analysis). I, in a sense, worked backwards from the objective to the subjective, reversing the steps on the "ladder" for dealing with the patient's transference dreams (see p. 130). Just as there is a mutuality of the unconscious wounds in the model suggested, so the dreams too may have more of a shared than a separate quality. And much like Jacoby's mention of a transference dream that "really belonged to us both" (1984, p. 33), countertransference dreams may also inhabit a mutual space, even at the beginning of treatment. The analyst here is relying on his unconscious being relatively "clean" and ready to provide information about the patient or situation from the outset. In the above case, regardless of where one puts the interpretive emphasis, it can be seen that my unconscious, heavily impacted by this penetrating client, was apparently trying to right the balance at various levels.

Finally, on the subject/object matter it is worthwhile to recall Fordham's early reminder that most patient statements are made to a projected figure (Fordham, 1957, p. 146). This applies equally to the therapist's statements. We are epistemologically bound, as Jung always pointed out, by the fact that the psyche itself is making statements about itself or another's psyche. The analyst always "imagines" things about the patient. Even what we see in sensate fashion before our eyes is subjectively determined and sometimes variable. And when it comes to something like a dream, the most detailed description, drawing or photograph (if it were possible) can only be recreated in the analyst's imagination, according to the analyst's subjective fantasies. When a patient tells a dream, the analyst supplies the visual picture.

Training analysis

The question of subjectivity brings up the issue of training analysis again. It goes without saying that it is vital in the context of a countertransference-based method. Also the point has already been made that, among other things, analysis yields a more ready access to feelings in depth rather than their elimination. Unmanageable "problems" or pathology should be relatively eliminated, though "eliminated" may not be the best word – perhaps "worked through" or, at a minimum, controlled. The analyst's unconscious may not be (indeed, cannot be) one that is totally clean or "cured," but one that can be trusted and that usually works for the analyst (and the patient). The fantasy of the therapist's invulnerability has to be dropped, since countertransference work, at least the "wounded healer" form described here, *relies* on the therapist's wounds in new or old editions.

In a manner of speaking, some degree of failure in training analysis may even be appropriate. Could it be said that one's inevitably incomplete analysis provides some of the impetus for continuing the work professionally? Or that modifications of theory or technique are sometimes attempted improvements on training analysis?[17] At any rate, the therapist may not be much less neurotic than the patient in certain ways, just more facile in his awareness. Analysts may project a little less than patients, and certainly catch or try to consider their "projectiles" before they go as far. One way they do this is by allowing a free flow, privately, of fantasies or feelings about patients. This elucidates the shadow, seems to correspond in remarkable ways with the patient's flow of thought and feeling (Dieckmann, 1976), and provides real ground for the "working through" of the now "mutual" unconscious process.

Jung's important statement that "An analyst can help his patient just so far as he himself has gone" (Jung, 1937, p. 330) is therefore not entirely true, at least as applied to training analysis. It should be remembered that Jung also wrote: "No analysis is capable of banishing all unconsciousness for ever. The analyst must go on learning endlessly" (Jung, 1951a, p. 116). Furthermore, by Jungian definition the unconscious is probably infinite, despite the familiar stopping points. Clearly, the training analysis cannot take one all the way. However, it can, aside from the actual work on the candidate's material, provide the model, integrity and spirit under which to continue the work via a lifelong self-analysis. Indeed, Jung mentions specifically not only the analyzed analyst but the analyst who "can bring such passion for the truth to the work that he can analyze himself through his patient" (Jung, 1921b, p. 137). Patients get into unknown places, unknown to the therapist too, and the latter will have to try to follow or else the patient will feel abandoned there. An analyst cannot have been everywhere, or have been there in the same way, but must be willing and able to accompany the patient. The patient's emotional vectors will come into the analyst regardless, via the countertransference.

Ongoing self-analysis is relevant, of course, to any analyst. When countertransference tends to be more the focus, however, a special premium is put on it. Supervision, formal or informal, can be a worthy adjunct, as can personal analysis at any time. Dieckmann's Berlin research project (1974, 1976) had a collegial processing group as a core component, which partly raises the question of its necessity for that kind of work. Jung, as I recall, somewhere prescribed a case confidante for the analyst, preferably (for him) with a well-developed feeling function and of the opposite sex.

Typology

This mention of "function" brings up the issue of typology in countertransference-based analysis. About half of Jungian analysts are not type-oriented in their work, at least not in any systematic or consistent way (Plaut, 1972)[18]. As envisioned in this book, countertransference work would naturally seem to involve superior intuitive and feeling tendencies. However, other type-linked characteristics or combinations can no doubt make countertransference workable in equal or better ways. Only a capacity for introspection would seem to be a prerequisite.

Thus the analyst's "type" per se does not seem to be the main thing. There may be therapists who have more "countertransference vulnerability" than others, but this would be a result of things other than typology. Jung, as mentioned, speaks of a "fateful disposition" or an "instinctive disposition" towards "psychic infections" (Jung, 1946, p. 177). Guggenbuhl-Craig suggests that there are "genuine 'wounded healers' among analysts" (Guggenbuhl-Craig, 1971, p. 129). As noted earlier, a good relationship with the "feminine" principle (as it is usually defined) might incline an analyst toward a countertransference orientation based on fusion, receptivity, eros, etc. Overall, there are "types" of analysts who, not so much due to typological function as other characterological reasons, lean more towards countertransference/ transference emphases. What Brown said about the sources of the Freud/Jung split – "It appears that Jungians and Freudians, like Liberals and Conservatives, are born and not made" (Brown, 1961, p. 43) – may apply here as well. "Countertransference" people may just be born that way. That is why there are "schools" of analysis in general, even within Jungian analysis, as Samuels (1985) has discussed.

Typology shows up more in *how* the therapist works with

countertransference issues rather than if he can. He will no doubt process his countertransference according to his typical ways of working through things. This would also be true in terms of different or similar patient/therapist types and the resulting effects on countertransference. There are different "kinds" of patients, each producing different countertransference responses, but the main thing is to follow the responses to that person, type included. There can be little doubt that, among other things, the analyst will react to a patient's style of processing and presenting things – his type. However, these typical modes can be characterized at a more specific level than the general, conscious plane typological analysis operates on. Again, "function"-type can be what Kohut terms an "experience-distant" (as opposed to "-near") manner of *thinking* about patients, whereas this book's emphasis is more towards empathy- or identification-based orientations. There is, of course, empathy in "rotating one's type" in order to fit a patient's, but this in part is an elaborate way of saying we try to listen to (and speak) the client's own language. A more fundamental dimension might be emotion, rather than typology. The strength of feelings toward or with a patient, and the various fluctuations thereof, leads out of typology and into the realm of complexes. The therapist may well respond more to types of complexes, so to speak, in the analytic field than to the psychological type of the patient per se[19].

Types of countertransference-inducing situations

The issue of type is most cogent in terms of the various types of countertransference-inducing *situations* that may arise in analysis. A number of these have been discussed here in the cases. The erotic countertransference was a key feature of case one (Ms. F), while some aspects of working with a more scared or scary (threatening, suicidal, more disturbed) patient came up in the second case. But no countertransference is simple or static, and each needs to evolve for the therapy to work (problems arising when countertransference remains frozen). Thus a full range of analyst reactions may ensue in each case. In light of this paper's "Jungian" orientation, one could say there are as many countertransferences as there are individual patients. Accepting, "seeing" and mirroring the patient's unique self is the necessary and often (the?) most therapeutic task of the analyst.

However, a therapist still can encounter and classify different sorts of patients and resultant countertransference effects (and affects). Countertransference-based work is in some ways a psychotherapy of impasse, of the analyst's getting stuck, "hooked" or fused with the patient's infectious, constellating unconscious. Therefore, most countertransference situations will be characterized by temporary or longer-term anxiety. And thus almost all countertransferences are manifestly or potentially difficult. As Jung said, in the same paragraph where he first mentioned the wounded healer's "own hurt" as a source of his power to heal: "Difficult cases are a veritable ordeal" (Jung, 1951a, p. 116).

An actual typology of countertransferences is not much discussed in the Jungian literature. M. Stein (1984, p. 71) points out that "maternal-nurturant" and "eros-sexual" patterns have been dealt with by Machtiger and Schwartz-Salant respectively. This is only partially true, as Machtiger has not really detailed this and Schwartz-Salant has his own in-depth but very specialized, subtle-body/inner-couples approach. Stein himself goes on to add "power, shamanism and maieutics" as countertransferences. However, it seems he is characterizing here certain analytic styles rather than countertransference-inducing situations per se. Keeping in mind that any case will give rise to certain countertransference reactions (even if one is not inclined to a countertransference focus), this section will note and provide brief examples of some other "typical" countertransference situations. Each of these situations, it should be noted, could almost merit its own book, and the list is, of course, not exhaustive.

Life crises in the therapist or his family not only limit his emotional resources but can call for difficult and sometimes fortuitous differentiations.

Example

When an elderly patient's husband died, this coincided with the death of my stepfather. Aside from my previous efforts to sort out this patient's personal realities from a maternal or even grandmotherly countertransference, I now had to struggle to differentiate her grief and grieving style from my own mother's (and my own). This three-way process, while complex and demanding, also enhanced my empathic range with the patient. The enhancement came not only from my

137

now personally deepened capacity to comprehend grief, but from an ability to understand my patient's style and speed of grieving based on my own mother's. That is, I began to see similarities in their modes of grieving and, as I also processed my filial impatience and various oedipal issues, I could use these to increase my understanding of my patient.

Suicidal feelings (in the patient) can generate intensely anxious countertransference responses in therapists. This was a some- what prominent feature of case two (Ms. J), alongside outwardly aggressive feelings. They do not receive much countertransference attention in Jungian literature, save for Jung's vivid parapsychological example of a patient who shot himself (Jung, 1961a, p. 137) and Machtiger's passing mention (Machtiger, 1982, p. 104).

Example

An aging male patient with pederastic (but platonic) and alcoholic tendencies, within a year lost his wife (to divorce) and was on the verge of losing an emotionally nourishing job. He spoke with relief about death and the life insurance his wife would receive. His father once tried to shoot himself with a gun the patient had and he (the patient) frequently yelled at himself, "You don't deserve to live!" He scored high as a suicide risk and, since past and present medication attempts had failed, a psychiatric consultant recommended electro-shock. Though committable, he said and (I felt too) that being hospitalized would "kill" him.

At various times this client generated in me: intense fear that he would suicide, helpless desperation (which I thought might be similar to his own), a desire to be rid of him (abandon him and my anxieties), an irritated impatience (at his masochistic, passive-aggressive manner), fear of lawsuits-shame-collegial condemnation, and more. Yet, this humiliated man, who denied homosexuality, wrote literally thousands of words a day (unpublished novels, mostly about youths) and fantasized that, in death, he would be united with a boy. It can be especially taxing when there are images of rebirth in the psyche alongside a possibly uncontainable despair. It was difficult, indeed impossible in this instance, for me to maintain a strictly symbolic stance with this patient[20].

Both of the above patients stimulated reactions that also had to do with our significant *age differences*, raising the issue of clients who may serve either as "countertransference parents" or "countertransference children" to the analyst.

Examples

The older female patient (p. 137) was not only twice my age, but I saw her potentially as a "wise old woman" who could clarify "the mysteries" of life and death for me. These issues were close at hand in the countertransference because my father, a close friend and my stepfather had recently died. She had had an unusual number of premature losses in her life: mother (very early divorce and separation from), father (suicide), brother, her only son, and second husband. During treatment her third husband and a grandson died. It was she, more than me, who had always needed a Mother: she almost directly asked for mirroring and dreamed of lost little girls who needed attention. Providing it involved my remembering that she could not solve *my* death and loss issues, which after all were specifically different. Second, it meant seeing the three-year-old in this woman twice my age. This was made more complex because I was the same age as her late son would have been. Thus the differentiation of this patient from my mother, which I referred to earlier, was accompanied by the differentiation of me from her son, her from the "great mother," and her losses from mine. In the countertransference she was child, mother, grandmother, wise old woman.

The second patient above, the man who loved "the boy," had some qualities that reminded me of my at one time depressed and divorced father, though other aspects were noticeably different. In contrast to the first patient, this one readily saw me as the "grown up," whereas he was an inept "boy." This dynamic was not unlike certain issues with my father. While almost all patients require the therapist to see the "child" in them, this may become taxing from a countertransference perspective when the patient is considerably older than the therapist. The reverse may be equally interesting though perhaps less demanding: when patients are literally young enough to remind one of (or "be") one's own children. I have not experienced this yet. However, the narcissistic demand that a patient of whatever age fulfill my ambitions, therapeutic hopes or dreams (or, alternatively, *not* surpass me) is familiar to me.

A common situation for Jungians is *mystical* or "new age" clients. A fair number of people are understandably attracted to Jung as a spiritual guide. Sometimes there is a tendency to overlook what Jung called "the shadow," or even severe pathology, in favor of extra-mundane pursuits. This may constitute a sort of "Jungian" defense against personal issues – the *prima materia* of analysis – or against the personal unconscious. These clients are among those "persons who enter Jungian analysis and are surprised to find that it is analytically tough-minded and mostly devoid of cultic or mystical qualities" (Stein, 1982, p. xv). Such patients sometimes tend to induce in me countertransferences of nostalgia (for the time when "Jung," for me, was Religion), envy, an eye-rolling cynicism about their spiritual quests, irony (to deflate pretentiousness), compensatory groundedness (one becomes *senex* to their *puer*), etc. – all of which may be quite informative.

Example

A young Oriental student sought help, he stated, because I was a "Jungian" and could deal with his spiritual and "psychopathological" issues. He had recently discovered that he was one of the "Star-born," a group of once lonely, now "special" people. This somewhat schizoid but sensitive individual had vivid psychic experiences and was involved in reincarnation, "channelling," and "fifth dimension" planes. However, his intelligence and Buddhist and philosophical background allowed him some detachment from his ideas. At times I was unsure, or worried, if he was "crazy" or not. Such attributions, it turned out, had been his lifelong experience with family and in the world.

I seemed to become for him (and within a complementary countertransference) the father, family and world who never understood him. Other times I served as the necessary reminder of ego and life in this world. When he once said to me in passing, "You're not 'spiritual'!" I bristled inwardly in protest, not wanting to be shut out from him and that possibility. When he undertook to criticize "people from the 60s" (like me) as compared to the "New Age" he felt part of, I felt impelled to straighten him out on the facts (protecting "my generation" and myself). Ultimately, to deflate this pomposity one time, I noted something like, "There's nothing you're mentioning here that people in the 60s, and indeed throughout this century and others, have not con- sidered." "Spiritual" materialism, I felt, is really no different than any other kind of competition (he was a business student).

However, for all the competition in the field, this person needed to feel unique and even to be hostile, for developmental and compensatory reasons. Wondering at times if he was potentially psychotic or just "different," I was forced to clarify just how much individual, spiritual and even cultural difference can be allowed for and empathized with.

As with the just described person, countertransferences to *hostility in patients* are as dependent on the situation and patient as any other. Some examples have been given already, in case two (Ms. J) and in this chapter (p. 131). Some patients are less obviously hostile, as in the earlier example of the older boy-man, and may provoke complementary, fear-based or frustrated *anger in the analyst*. It seems appropriate not to vent this on the patient, despite some anecdotal evidence to the contrary and Jung's trademark spontaneity: "I expose myself completely and react with no restriction" (Jung, 1935a, p. 139).

Example

After considerable self-containment with a resistant and consistently acting-out patient, I tried what I hoped might be a daring, Zen masterstroke by saying with real force, "What do you think this is, a goddamn joke?!" Justifying all this as "information" for her, I also revealed that her behaviors had engendered fantasies in me of kicking her out of analysis. This patient ultimately terminated under extremely hostile circumstances which included an attempt at blackmail. The retaliatory aspect of my attempted "shock" therapy probably hastened the process.

141

In retrospect, it would have been better to have contained the anger she induced, or let off the necessary steam in some way (irony perhaps, as I had done with the verbally abusive patient on p. 132). Fordham gives an example of an aggravating patient who asked him if he had said "karma or calmer?" – to which Fordham (rather snidely, I think) joked and spelled out "kalmer" (1978a, p. 129). But basically the non-retaliatory, non-"talion" response Lambert (1972) recommends seems preferable. Winnicott's idea (1949) about objective "hate in the countertransference" – justifiable feelings which can sometimes be revealed to the patient much later, when he is well – is very relevant to this discussion. On the opposite pole is Searles who, to avoid the build-up of resentment and guilt, is resolved to "give as good as I get, hour by hour" with his often rather severely disturbed clientele (Searles, 1966, p. 34).

Self-disclosure

All this on retaliation has to do with the broader question of disclosure of countertransference by the analyst. This topic too is difficult to discuss outside of particular contexts and individuals. By and large it feels better, for me personally, to err on the side of reserve. Jung evidently took a "fire away!" position, as evidenced by his Tavistock comments[21] and first-person reports of his uncanny, intuitive powers and charismatic personality (see Jaffé, 1971). His countertransference dream of the client in the "castle tower" was one he immediately revealed and interpreted to the patient, with reportedly beneficial results (Jung, 1943, p. 112). For analysts with a less dynamic personal "presence," careful study of the situation may be in order.

The psychoanalysts, who have studied this situation longer, fall roughly into three "disclosure" camps: conservative (none), moderate (selective expression) and radical (freer, though not thoughtless use)[22]. This is a useful spectrum, upon which one need not be fixed. One's position on it could conceivably vary from session to session, or even within a session. It would much depend, again, on the client, therapeutic alliance, timing, atmosphere, associations, intuitions, empathic states, length or stage of treatment – it is one of the many decisions referred to in the earlier "paradigm" section of this chapter.

Still, a general standpoint can be ascertained. Jung would probably fall on the radical end of the scale. My position would be more moderate to conservative: if disclosure is called for, it might usually be limited to in-session feeling states or bits of countertransferences that are well worked through. That is, it is better to show "end results" of countertransference-based work than "still in process" detail. Under-metabolized reactions may be consciously interesting but primarily a burden to the already burdened patient. They tend to invite analysis of the analyst, which the patient shouldn't need to do, is really not equipped to do and may resent. Not that the patient or his unconscious are not monitoring or perhaps, as Searles suggests, trying to "cure" the analyst. The analyst should take the cues, in my view, but keep the responsibility. If something is to be "shared" from the countertransference, then it might best come from a relatively neutral stance, if possible, rather than being full of emotion. A good safeguard is to check the state of one's arousal when moving to disclose.

Of course it is often impossible to find that "neutral" place, or a patient may press or challenge the therapist. Honesty must be the best policy, but honesty does not necessarily mean vast disclosure. It may mean limited, tactful or no disclosure. It seems basically appropriate to keep quiet when unsure, but alright to admit error or unsureness when that is the situation and it can be done non-defensively. Within the context of a session an image, feeling or association can be shared. The details, however, can be left out. And in general it seems correct that such reactions should come as responses or furtherances of something the patient is currently saying, so the disclosure is more an amplifying reaction than an active, directive comment. On the other hand, sometimes the process must simply be contained, or the "field" (as Goodheart puts it) may be a "complex-discharging" one in which there is nothing much to be said. The hope then is that the working or therapeutic alliance is intact enough to sustain the chaotic unconscious states.

At the other end of the disclosure continuum is Schwartz-Salant's idea of the importance of validating the patient's (especially the borderline patient's) "vision" of the analyst. As usual, this complicated issue depends much on the client's sophistication and the specific context, as well as the accuracy of the perception. The maturity of the analytic relationship would also be a key factor. Likewise Schwartz-Salant's very free participation and sharing in the imaginal field would seem to require a lengthy development and a special relationship. For instance,

143

while this passage is taken out of its "imaginal" context, it would be difficult for me to actually tell a patient, "I want to penetrate you from the rear" (Schwartz-Salant, 1986, p. 44). Now it may be he is deep within an "in vivo," erotic field that others are less able to enter in session. Nevertheless, the model delineated in this paper also involves a full recognition of these sorts of analyst fantasies, but in a private, usually undisclosed domain.

Along these same lines, some care needs to be taken with the more intuitive realizations an analyst may come to, whether through direct use of countertransference or dreams. The self-disclosure issue is paramount here, as the effect can be strong. It is gratifying to all involved for the therapist to be seen as insightful or even a wizard of some sort. However, the chief question is one of timing, or what the patient needs. The great art in analysis is to "shut up." Flash insights must sometimes be held until the patient is ready for them, or sacrificed altogether. In my view, it doesn't hurt to count to ten and it is, moreover, important to double-check one's intuition. Fordham (1978a) has urged caution about quick countertransference-based revelations to patients – one must wait until the patient's material catches up with what the analyst already "knows."

At a general level, countertransference work boils down to a two-part sequence: processing it and then doing something with it. As Rosemary Gordon states: after differentiating the material, the analyst must then "decide whether to communicate to the patient his emotional reactions and, if so, in what form and when" (Gordon, 1968, p. 181). Although he occupies a place on the more radical side of the self-disclosure debate, Searles seems to sum up accurately the intangible bases for answering this question of when and how to reveal countertransference material:

> It is clear to me that the analyst's *inner freedom to experience* feelings, fantasies and patient-transference-related shifts in his personal identity . . . is unequivocally desirable and necessary. But it is equally clear that only his therapeutic intuition, grounded in his accumulating clinical experience, can best instruct him when it is timely and useful – and when, on the other hand, it is ill timed and injudicious – to *express* these inner experiences.
>
> (Searles, 1973, p. 279)

This entire matter of self-disclosure may hinge not just on style and circumstance but on judgments about the importance of "identification" with the analyst. For many analysts the healing dynamic of the patient/therapist interaction is that the patient introjects a "good object," or experiences in the present a positive, "corrective emotional experience." But how this is achieved, or how this is imagined to happen, may determine the extent of explicit countertransference disclosure. As we are not sure about what precisely it is that "heals," there will naturally be variations in how a therapist deals day-to-day with the analytic relationship. Without trying to sound mysterious, it is my sense that the whole analytic process, including the basic nature of communication, is as much unconscious as conscious (which does not mean we do not need to nurse it along carefully and consciously). Accordingly, in terms of countertransference, self-knowledge seems more vital than self-disclosure per se. It is possible to be radical in feeling and conservative in revealing. Since there can probably be no set rule on self-disclosure, the main thing would be a continuous consideration of the matter, in general and in the particular instance.

The shadow of countertransference

Countertransference, which historically was thought to be what Jungians would call "shadow" (in a negative sense), always will have a shadow. Everything of substance does, including any technique or style of doing analysis. Shadow is created by light, and any focusing of consciousness or light will deepen shadow and leave other things out of the picture. As Guggenbuhl-Craig (1968, p. 251) has suggested, consciousness *creates* unconsciousness. The dangers of this kind of countertransference-based work have been reckoned with throughout this book, directly or indirectly. Safeguards have been discussed. However, it is appropriate in closing to address further this issue of "the shadow of countertransference."

Working with the foggy, intermingling aspects of countertransference/transference requires loosening the boundaries between people somewhat more than if one experiences analysis as a "separate" activity. In a fused situation, there is always the potential for complication. By attending to and "participating" in the conscious and unconscious analytic interaction, the risks are greater and the complexity is greater – also the healing potential may sometimes be greater.

A principal danger here is the so-called "neurotic counter-transference" in the classic sense. The personal equation can never be fully mastered or wholly anticipated, even with thorough or ongoing analysis, supervision, etc. Thus "pathology" in the analyst can always arise. Indeed, in this model it should arise, or at least the analyst should get stuck periodically. Working within a countertransference orientation, there are fewer protections against such dangers or blind spots than when, by technique or viewpoint, the analyst is more distant from the process.

Added to this is the danger that arises from characterizing countertransferences as "mixed," rather than plainly neurotic or clearly informative. If pursued at all, countertransference has to be pursued through this cloudy area of "hooks," "reality nuclei," "objective" dreams, the patient's unconscious monitoring and his accurate "imaginal perceptions." And because it is not "either-or," countertransference has to be pursued continuously. This forms the basis of the method, of course, but one is on the horns of this not easily resolved dilemma at all times. Where one tends to go is into a new paradigm altogether, where the idea of the "this or that" (e.g. neurotic or informative) is temporarily left behind.

Jung referred to this transcendence of the tension of opposites in the transference as the "the transformation of the third" (1946, p. 199), and Schwartz-Salant has furthered Jung's alchemical concepts and described the experiences vividly. Here, the dilemma of "mixed" countertransferences becomes transcended in a kind of paradigm shift. This synthetic resolution is not necessarily a problem; however, it should be noted that the radical shift in orientation can be disconcerting, and requires considerable flexibility in the participants.

The countertransference situation is shot through with induced feelings in addition to the neurotic, mixed or quasi-transcendent ones just mentioned. The risks for patient and therapist alike of the necessary psychic infections are great. This can be a therapy of maximum impact, and the question must always be asked, "Who is inducing whom?" The transcendent mode, above, goes past this question, inviting study instead of the conjoined field. Stein (1984, p. 78) warns that such "shamanistic" ventures run the risk of "folie à deux" and reversal of therapeutic direction (the patient curing the analyst). This is indeed the tightrope walked by the "wounded-healer" type of analyst. Its dangers and concomitant responsibilities must not be underestimated.

CONCLUSIONS

Fools rush in. Of course, Freud (1913) admitted that his "neutral" analytic ideal and techniques had many self-protective, counter-countertransference components[23]. Jung (1946) jumped on Freud for this, accurately catching and criticizing the cool *shadow* of Freudian technique. However, Freud probably meant well and was trying to deal with the personal, professional and public relations dangers of his theory. Meanwhile, Jung pushed the edge bravely but did fall victim to the very dangers noted here – he seemed to have crossed over the line with some of his patients[24].

Other high-level dangers are inherent in this type of work. As Jung demonstrated (as the first case, Ms. F, here did also), the therapist's intimacy needs can easily come into play. It is, again, inevitable that the therapist working via himself will bring his whole self to the treatment. Needs must be known, fulfilled elsewhere if possible, or sometimes sacrificed. This is not fun. Furthermore, countertransference/transference work as a whole impinges on and confronts the incest question quite directly. One is working against personal and collective taboo in a perilous zone of fundamental human mystery and the most complex emotions, in depth. As Jungian analyst A. Hill has pointed out (personal communication), this exerts a "profound" pull on analysts: "We long for incest as much as our clients." For, as Jung also points out, "Incest symbolizes union with one's own being, it means individuation or becoming a self" (Jung, 1946, p. 218).

In addition, there is always the possibility of self-deception, in a countertransference-based style of analysis or any other. Being too attached to any one format can be problematic. The cases presented in this book could be approached in other ways or with other emphases – with positive effect. Therefore, a further shadow dimension of this style has to do with ideas of reference (in the analyst). By attending to transference dynamics, the analyst may tend exclusively to refer the patient's material to the analytic situation per se or the analyst. Similarly, for the analyst to focus only on countertransference could represent a narcissistic problem. One needs to come in and out of the self-preoccupation of countertransference analysis – working properly, the therapist shifts constantly between his subjective reactions (countertransference) and his imaginings about how the client feels (empathy). These are very intricately interwoven.

A pluralistic standpoint (Samuels, 1989) is not only truthful to

147

the multiple reference points of psychic reality, it is useful. Just as a countertransference reaction can be looked at in many ways, so can transference or any patient material. This is something like Jung's mention of the "wavicle" theory of light – it is both wave and particle, *both* are true (Jung, 1947, p. 229). So one must stretch one's mind out to possibilities, and then let go sometimes as well.

These then are some of the dangers of countertransference work. There are no doubt other problems. A countertransference focus is inherently an area of unsureness, lack of clarity, and subject/object confusion. All in all, though, it may not be any more subject to these dangers than other methods. The fantasy that issues of countertransference are not in play in non-countertransference styles of working is not tenable. On the other hand, to focus primarily on one's own inner process can run the risk of missing or downplaying the patient's. However, it is not an exclusive method, and has not been presented here as such. A major portion of Jung's theory and style (what we know of it), the work of the SAP school, Dieckmann's research, indeed all of the writers noted in the review – they all rely heavily on it, each with a personal variation that makes sense. Basic Jungian principles about mutual transformation and participation of the analyst, the mysterious communicative range of the psyche and the purposive-prospective nature of the unconscious are fundamentally involved. Even the most "neurotic" countertransference can also contain, as Jung said of the patient's neurosis, "the true gold we should never have found elsewhere" (Jung, 1934a, p. 170).

To get at the gold, one works in a slightly different manner than originally thought. I have tried to elucidate here a way of doing that, a way to work with countertransference as a central dimension. In keeping with Jungian principles, it is a two-way street between analyst and patient; but also a two-way operation within the analyst, involving separating and fusing at the same time. It moves in a decidedly paradoxical realm, and rests on certain shifts of perspective that have been outlined here. One works "closer to the bone" or, like some matadors, closer to the bull (in many senses, sometimes). A better metaphor would be that the analyst really does straddle a line between sickness and health in this experience-based mode of working. I find it natural and meaningful to work and conceptualize in this way, under the aegis of the wounded-healer archetype.

NOTES

1 INTRODUCTION

1 See also Racker (1953, 1957), Tower (1956).
2 Fordham et al.'s (1974) collection of London-based technical perspectives and Jacoby's (1984) book of lectures on the "analytic encounter" do examine this topic in some depth, though not exclusively.
3 See *Symbols of Transformation* (1911–12/1952), *The Visions Seminars* (1930–34), "A Study in the Process of Individuation" (1934b), "Individual Dream Symbolism in Relation to Alchemy" (1936) as examples.
4 The index to Jung's *Collected Works* has no listings under "Counter-transference." Instead the reader is referred to the "Transference" section, where it is cited only eight times. Nor do the *C.G. Jung: Letters* or his autobiography index the topic of countertransference. His definitive work on the analyst/patient interaction, "The Psychology of the Transference," uses the word as such just three times.
5 Jung's apparent reluctance to use the word "countertransference" may be similar to this downplaying of transference in the impromptu Tavistock Lectures: perhaps in both instances a reaction to Freud's terminology and overemphasis, as Jung saw it, on sexuality.
6 Within the same initial paragraph of his foreword to "The Psychology of the Transference," Jung states that "almost all cases requiring lengthy treatment gravitate around it" – before going on to add, "its importance is relative" (Jung, 1946, p. 164).

2 JUNGIAN APPROACHES TO COUNTERTRANSFERENCE: A REVIEW

1 See, for example, Wickes (1938), Baynes (1940), Adler (1961).
2 This journal supplements the quarterly *Journal of Analytical Psychology* (1955–), the first Jungian journal with a primarily clinical focus. Since the 1970s, the London group has published collections of clinical studies in book form as well.

3 Ferenczi was apparently moving in this direction in 1918 in "The Control of the Countertransference."
4 I will be using the masculine pronoun throughout this thesis, when speaking generally.
5 As Samuels (1985) points out, this redefinition has not been widely accepted.
6 This, in reverse, is what an analyst may frequently hear from his patients, interestingly enough.
7 Moody's (1955) excellent case example is groundbreaking more in terms of showing his active participation than his unconscious fantasies.
8 Jung's story of the Rainmaker goes as follows:

> As an example of "being in Tao" and its synchronistic accompaniments I will cite the story, told me by the late Richard Wilhelm, of the rain-maker of Kiao-chau: "There was a great drought where Wilhelm lived; for months there hadn't been a drop of rain and the situation became catastrophic. The Catholics made processions, the Protestants made prayers, and the Chinese burned joss-sticks and shot off guns to frighten off the demons of the drought, but with no result. Finally the Chinese said, 'We will fetch the rain-maker.' And from another province a dried up old man appeared. The only thing he asked for was a quiet little house somewhere, and there he locked himself in for three days. On the fourth day the clouds gathered and there was a great snow-storm at the time of the year when no snow was expected, an unusual amount, and the town so full of rumours about the wonderful rain-maker that Wilhelm went to ask the man how he did it. In true European fashion he said: 'They call you the rain-maker, will you tell me how you made the snow?' And the little Chinese said: 'I did not make the snow, I am not responsible.' 'But what have you done these three days?' 'Oh, I can explain that. I come from another country where things are in order. Here they are out of order, they are not as they should be by the ordinance of heaven. Therefore the whole country is not in Tao, and I also am not in the natural order of things because I am in a disordered country. So I had to wait three days until I was back in Tao and then naturally the rain came.'"
>
> (Jung, 1955–56, pp. 419–420n)

9 C.A. Meier's 1949/1967 book, *Ancient Incubation and Modern Psychotherapy*, explores Asklepian healing practices in a most informative way, and is an excellent background source for this line of thought. However, as Samuels points out, "There is little in this book concerning what we would now call countertransference" (Samuels, 1985, p. 187).
10 See, however, Smith, Glass and Miller's now classic research study, *The Benefits of Psychotherapy* (1981), which statistically shows that therapy, and presumably analysis, "works."

11 See Searles on "using the patient to bear the burden of all the severe psychopathology in the whole relationship" (1978, pp. 62–63).

12 This question, "Why had I. . . ", appears in the original version of Parks' paper, presented at a conference in 1986, on page 16. It is deleted from the published version in the *Journal of Analytical Psychology*.

13 Though somewhat similar, this notion still seems fundamentally different than: 1) the idea of projection "hooks," 2) Fordham's idea of "deintegrating" to meet the patient's disintegration (1957, p. 143), or 3) Lambert's idea of complementary countertransferences becoming concordant (1972, p. 313).

3 CASE ILLUSTRATIONS

1 See Searles (1967, p. 24) for a similar concept, though it is not quite clear if he is referring to imaginal activity at the beginning of treatment.

2 My feeling these days is almost always that I have committed some sort of violation when I disclose to a patient. It feels wrong to me, somehow. This is not to say this position is universally correct – just correct for me, as I feel it.

3 The cancer under my arm was a small skin cancer. My father, step-father and a close friend had died within a short span of time.

4 See Gendlin (1978) for explication of this concept, though in a somewhat different context.

5 One thinks here of Winnicott's tolerance for certain patients' acting out *on* his office. See, for instance, Margaret Little's memoir of her analysis (Little, 1991).

4 CONCLUSIONS

1 Groesbeck (1978) discusses in detail his working through of counter-transference dreams. An example of a countertransference dream can be found in Singer (1973, p. 325).

2 This is not meant to indicate a moral failure. However, it is evidence of a lack of depth in published countertransference studies. Natural anxieties about patient confidentiality, self-revelation and protecting the profession are less persuasive, in my opinion, than concerns about patients who might be upset by reading about complex countertransference states. This latter worry is outweighed by the fact that countertransference discussion is meant for, and apt to be read by, clinicians.

3 A good case can be made that effective use of the countertransference may involve what Jungians often term the "feminine" principle.

4 There appear to be only three papers in which Freud's views on countertransference are briefly delineated (Freud 1910, 1912, 1915) and one, "Analysis Terminable and Interminable" (1937), where periodic, further analysis of the analyst is recommended.

5 One can be "blank" or numb or schizoid or whatever as part and parcel of a countertransference position however.

6 I am not speaking here to the issue of analyst self-disclosure, which is another topic altogether.

7 I believe Winnicott and/or Bion point this out.

8 The general idea here about the ego-self axis in the countertransference context comes from A. Hill (personal communication), though the idea about the necessity of getting "lost" is this author's.

9 Searles in fact says this well: "Interpretations are important, to be sure, but of far greater importance is the emotional atmosphere or climate of the sessions, day after day, year after year" (1978, p. 44).

10 I would not regard these as really separate.

11 As I discovered in retrospect, this model in some ways and even in some wordings resembles Tansey and Burke's (1989) comprehensive, if somewhat surgical, model. When attempting to describe countertransference processes in detail, overlap between authors is inevitable.

12 Somehow these active, even military metaphors seem to flow forth here, perhaps related to anxieties one feels about having personal "territory" or boundaries crossed.

13 Sadly, one must take into account liability considerations here.

14 I have often noticed that, after I make an interpretation, I sometimes shift my body position. This could indicate: release, defense, punctuation, separation from a fusion, etc. It is as if the body were holding the interpretation, or the words.

15 As Searles dramatically states, the analyst is

> in the grips of a process . . . [which is] far too powerful for either the patient or himself to be able at all to deflect it, consciously and willfully and singlehandedly, away from the confluent channel which it is tending – with irresistible power, if we can give ourselves up to the current – to form for itself.
>
> (Searles, 1961, p. 559)

Casement puts it less lyrically:

> The analyst aims to be the servant of the analytic process, not its master . . . . The analyst's effectiveness is best demonstrated through learning to follow the analytic process, not in trying to control it. And when the analytic space is most clearly preserved for the patient . . . the analytic process can be seen to have a life of its own. Where it might lead cannot be anticipated.
>
> (Casement, 1991, p. 345)

16 Re-reading Racker recently, I found still another interesting possibility:

> Owing to the prohibition of active-phallic impulses both in the past oedipal situation and in the present analytical situation . . . these feelings and impulses easily acquire a passive-phallic character. The unconscious desire may now be (at this level) that the patient should fall in love with the analyst's penis.
>
> (Racker, 1953, p. 108)

It is not clear, of course, whether Racker is here referring to himself or to other analysts as well.

17 Winnicott (1949, p. 70) alludes to this, as does Langs (Langs and Searles 1980) in terms of writing. Jungian analyst Alex McCurdy once remarked at a conference that after training one can begin one's analysis; Fordham (1978a, p. 163) raises the same question.

18 Typological analysis itself may require a "thinking" orientation, because it attempts to be logical and organized. However, that conclusion may be a function of this author's inferior thinking.

19 Quenk and Quenk (1982) and Beebe (1984) have good articles on typology and the analytic relationship, though only Beebe begins to touch on countertransference dimensions. These authors clearly have a better developed relationship to typology in general than I have.

The only real discussion of countertransference and type is Groesbeck's "Psychological Types in the Analysis of Transference" (1978), which I found after this chapter was written. While this excellent article discusses mismatches and "rotation" of types in analyst and patient, its most important parts (for me) relate to the value of analytic "failure" and the constellation thereby of an archetypal "inner healer." His case examples are specifically about countertransference "wounds" (again, going beyond typology as such in my opinion). Countertransference dreams are discussed and worked through for the first time since Jung's example (1937).

20 This patient was ultimately "saved," through no particular help of mine (though I did stand by him at the crucial time): an excellent position luckily opened up for him. He quit his longtime job, which he was doomed to lose anyway, and moved on and ultimately remarried.

Hillman's provocative meditation on suicide, *Suicide and the Soul* (1964), is perhaps relevant to this case.

21 Again, Jung's seemingly piqued emotional state at that lecture may have some bearing on the forcefulness of his statements (Jung, 1935a, p. 139).

22 See Gorkin (1987) and Tansey and Burke (1989) for a good survey and discussion of this classification.

23 See Freud (1913, 1915). Freud's frank reservations about being seen by patients – "I cannot bear to be gazed at for eight hours a day" (1913, p. 146) – have been interestingly analyzed by Kohut (1977) in terms of their narcissistic dimension.

24 Jungian analyst Judy Savage has brought to my attention a thought-provoking article by Carotenuto (1990), which suggests that Freud's viewpoint (not to mention Jung's) on countertransference was heavily influenced by the Spielrein affair.

REFERENCES

Adler, G. (1961) *The Living Symbol*, Princeton: Princeton University Press.
—— (ed.) (1974) *Success and Failure in Analysis*, New York: Putnam's.
Baynes, H.G. (1940) *Mythology of the Soul*, London: Rider. [Re-published in 1955 by Routledge and Kegan Paul.]
Beebe, J. (1984) "Psychological Types in Transference, Countertransference, and the Therapeutic Interaction", *Chiron*, 1984: 147–161.
Blomeyer, R. (1974) "The Constellation of the Countertransference in Relation to the Presentation of Archetypal Dreams: Clinical Aspects", in Adler, G. (ed.) *Success and Failure in Analysis*, New York: Putnam's.
Brown, J.A.C. (1961) *Freud and the Post-Freudians*, Baltimore, Penguin Books.
Cameron, A. (1968) "Transference as Creative Illusion", in Fordham, M. *et al.* (eds) *Technique in Jungian Analysis*, London: Heinemann, 1974.
Campbell, R. (1967) "The Management of the Countertransference Evoked by Violence in the Delusional Transference", in Fordham, M. *et al.* (eds) *Technique in Jungian Analysis*, London: Heinemann, 1974.
Carotenuto, A. (1990) "Jung's Confrontation with Sabina Spielrein. Towards New Territories. Part II", *Psychologist Psychoanalyst*, 10: 9–16.
Casement, P. (1991) *Learning from the Patient*, New York: Guilford Press.
Charlton, R. (1986) "Free Association and Jungian Analytic Technique", *Journal of Analytical Psychology*, 31: 153–171.
Cohen, M.B. (1952) "Countertransference and Anxiety", *Psychiatry*, 15: 231–243.
Davidson, D. (1966) "Transference as a Form of Active Imagination", in Fordham, M. *et al.* (eds) *Technique in Jungian Analysis*, London: Heinemann, 1974.
Dieckmann, H. (1974) "The Constellation of the Countertransference in Relation to the Presentation of Archetypal Dreams: Research Methods and Results", in Adler, G. (ed.) *Success and Failure in Analysis*, New York: Putnam's.
—— (1976) "Transference and Countertransference: Results of a Berlin Research Group", *Journal of Analytical Psychology*, 12: 25–35.
Ellenberger, H. (1970) *The Discovery of the Unconscious*, New York: Basic Books.

154

REFERENCES

Epstein, L. and Feiner, A. (1979) *Countertransference: The Therapist's Contribution to the Therapeutic Process*, New York: Aronson.

Evans, R. (1976) *Jung on Elementary Psychology*, New York: Dutton.

Fordham, M. (1957) "Notes on the Transference", in Fordham, M. *et al.* (eds) *Technique in Jungian Analysis*, London: Heinemann, 1974.

—— (1960) "Countertransference", in Fordham, M. *et al.* (eds) *Technique in Jungian Analysis*, London: Heinemann, 1974.

—— (1969) "Technique and Countertransference", in Fordham, M. *et al.* (eds) *Technique in Jungian Analysis*, London: Heinemann, 1974.

—— (1978a) *Jungian Psychotherapy*, New York: John Wiley.

—— (1978b) "Some Idiosyncratic Behaviors of Therapists", *Journal of Analytical Psychology*, 23: 123–129.

—— (1979) "Analytical Psychology and Countertransference", *Contemporary Psychoanalysis*, 15: 630–646.

Fordham, M., Gordon, R., Hubback, J. and Lambert, K. (eds)(1974) *Technique in Jungian Analysis*, London: Heinemann.

Frantz, K. (1971) "The Analyst's Own Involvement with the Process and the Patient", in Wheelwright, J. (ed.) *The Analytic Process*, New York: Putnam's.

Freud, S. (1910) "The Future Prospects of Psychoanalytic Therapy", *Therapy and Technique*, New York: Collier, 1963.

—— (1912) "Recommendations for Physicians on the Psychoanalytic Method of Treatment", *Therapy and Technique*, New York: Collier, 1963.

—— (1913) "Further Recommendations in the Technique of Psychoanalysis: On Beginning the Treatment. The Question of the First Communications. The Dynamics of the Cure", *Therapy and Technique*, New York: Collier, 1963.

—— (1915) "Further Recommendations in the Technique of Psychoanalysis: Notes on Transference Love", *Therapy and Technique*, New York: Collier, 1963.

—— (1922) "Some Neurotic Mechanisms in Jealousy, Paranoia and Homosexuality", *Standard Edition of the Collected Works of Sigmund Freud*, Volume 18, London: Hogarth, 1955.

—— (1937) "Analysis Terminable and Interminable", *Therapy and Technique*, New York: Collier, 1963.

Gendlin, E. (1978) *Focusing*, New York: Everest House.

Goodheart, W.B. (1980) "Theory of Analytic Interaction", *Library Journal of the C.G. Jung Institute of San Francisco*, 1: 1–39.

—— (1984) "Successful and Unsuccessful Interventions in Jungian Analysis: The Construction and Destruction of the Spellbinding Circle", *Chiron*, 1984: 89–117.

—— (1985) "Comments", *Spring*, 1985: 161–164.

Gordon, R. (1968) "Transference as the Fulcrum of Analysis", in Fordham, M. *et al.* (eds) *Technique in Jungian Analysis*, London: Heinemann, 1974.

Gorkin, M. (1987) *The Uses of Countertransference*, New York: Aronson.

Groesbeck, C.J. (1975) "The Archetypal Image of the Wounded Healer", *Journal of Analytical Psychology*, 20: 122–145.

—— (1978) "Psychological Types in the Analysis of Transference", *Journal of Analytical Psychology*, 23: 23–53.

Guggenbuhl-Craig, A. (1968) "The Psychotherapist's Shadow", in Wheelwright, J. (ed.) *The Reality of the Psyche*, New York: Putnam's.

—— (1971) *Power in the Helping Professions*, Zurich: Spring Publications.

Hall, J. (1984) "Dreams and Transference/Countertransference: The Transformative Field", *Chiron*, 1984: 31–51.

Harms, E. (1962) "C.G. Jung", *American Journal of Psychiatry*, 118: 728–732.

Heimann, P. (1950) "On Countertransference", *International Journal of Psychoanalysis*, 31: 81–84.

Hillman, J. (1964) *Suicide and the Soul*, New York: HarperCollins, 1973.

Hubback, J. (1986) "Body Language and the Self: The Search for Psychic Truth", *Chiron*, 1986: 127–143.

Jacoby, M. (1971) "A Contribution to the Phenomenon of Transference", in Wheelwright, J. (ed.) *The Analytic Process*, New York: Putnam's.

—— (1981) "Reflections on Heinz Kohut's Concept of Narcissism", *Journal of Analytical Psychology*, 26: 19–32.

—— (1984) *The Analytic Encounter: Transference and Human Relationship*, Toronto: Inner City Books.

—— (1986) "Getting in Touch and Touching in Analysis", *Chiron*, 1986: 109–126.

—— (1990) *Individuation and Narcissism: The Psychology of Self in Jung and Kohut*, London: Routledge.

Jaffé, A. (1971) *From the Life and Work of C.G. Jung*, New York: HarperCollins.

Jung, C.G. (1953–1979) *The Collected Works of C.G. Jung*, H. Read, M. Fordham, G. Adler and W. McGuire (eds), 20 Volumes, Bollingen Series XX, Princeton: Princeton University Press. [Hereafter this collection will be referred to as *CW* with volume number.]

—— (1911–12/1952) *Symbols of Transformation*, CW 5.

—— (1913) "The Theory of Psychoanalysis", CW 4.

—— (1914) "Some Crucial Points in Psychoanalysis: A Correspondence Between Dr. Jung and Dr. Loy", CW 4.

—— (1921a) *Psychological Types*, CW 6.

—— (1921b) "The Therapeutic Value of Abreaction", CW 16.

—— (1928) "Child Development and Education", CW 17.

—— (1929a) "Problems of Modern Psychotherapy", CW 16.

—— (1929b) "Freud and Jung: Contrasts", CW 4.

—— (1930–34) *The Visions Seminars*, New York: Spring, 1976.

—— (1933) "The Meaning of Psychology for Modern Man", CW 10.

—— (1934a) "The State of Psychotherapy Today", CW 10.

—— (1934b) "A Study in the Process of Individuation", CW 9i.

—— (1935a) "The Tavistock Lectures", CW 18.

—— (1935b) "The Principles of Practical Psychotherapy", CW 16.

—— (1936) "Individual Dream Symbolism in Relation to Alchemy", CW 12.

—— (1937) "The Realities of Practical Psychotherapy", CW 16.

—— (1939) "The Symbolic Life", CW 18.

—— (1943) "On the Psychology of the Unconscious", CW 7.

—— (1946) "The Psychology of the Transference", *CW 16*.

—— (1947) "On the Nature of the Psyche", *CW 8*.

—— (1950) "Concerning Mandala Symbolism", *CW 8*.

—— (1951a) "Fundamental Questions of Psychotherapy", *CW 16*.

—— (1951b) *Aion, CW 9ii*.

—— (1955–56) *Mysterium Coniunctionis, CW 14*.

—— (1958) "Forward to the Swiss Edition", *CW 16*.

—— (1961a) *Memories, Dreams, Reflections*, New York: Vintage Books.

—— (1961b) "Symbols and The Interpretation of Dreams", *CW 18*.

—— (1973a) *Psychological Reflections*, Princeton: Princeton University Press.

—— (1973b) *Letters*, Volume 1, Adler, G. (ed.), Princeton: Princeton University Press.

—— (1977) "The Face to Face Interview", in McGuire, W. and Hull, R.F.C. (eds) *C.G. Jung Speaking*, Princeton: Princeton University Press.

Kernberg, O. (1965) "Notes on Countertransference", *Journal of the American Psychoanalytic Association*, 13: 38–56.

Kohut, H. (1971) *The Analysis of the Self*, New York: International Universities Press.

—— (1977) *The Restoration of the Self*, New York: International Universities Press.

Kugler, P. and Hillman, J. (1985) "The Autonomous Psyche: A Communication to Goodheart from the Bi-Personal Field of Paul Kugler and James Hillman", *Spring*, 1985: 141–185.

Lambert, K. (1972) "Transference/Countertransference: Talion Law and Gratitude", in Fordham, M. *et al.* (eds) *Technique in Jungian Analysis*, London: Heinemann, 1974.

—— (1976) "Resistance and Counter-resistance", *Journal of Analytical Psychology*, 21: 164–192.

Laing, R.D. (1976) *The Facts of Life*, New York: Pantheon.

Langs, R. (ed.) (1990) *Classics in Psychoanalytic Technique*, New York: Aronson.

Langs, R. and Searles, H. (1980) *Intrapsychic and Interpersonal Dimensions of Treatment*, New York: Aronson.

Little, M. (1951) "Countertransference and the Patient's Response to It", *International Journal of Psychoanalysis*, 32: 32–40.

—— (1991) *Psychotic Anxieties and Containment*, New York: Aronson.

McCurdy, A. (1982) "Establishing the Analytic Structure", in Stein, M. (ed.) *Jungian Analysis*, Boulder: Shambhala.

Machtiger, H. (1982) "Countertransference/Transference", in Stein, M. (ed.) *Jungian Analysis*, Boulder: Shambhala.

Masterson, J. (ed.) (1978) *New Perspectives on the Psychotherapy of the Borderline Adult*, New York: Brunner/Mazel.

—— (1983) *Countertransference and Psychotherapeutic Technique*, New York: Aronson.

Meier, C.A. (1949/1967) *Ancient Incubation and Modern Psychotherapy*, Evanston: Northwestern University Press.

Miller, A. (1981) *Prisoners of Childhood*, New York: Basic Books.

Moody, R. (1955) "On the Function of Countertransference", *Journal of Analytical Psychology*, 1: 49–58.

Newman, K.D. (1980) "Countertransference and Consciousness", *Spring*, 1980: 117–127.

Parks, S. (1987) "Experiments in Appropriating a New Way of Listening", *Journal of Analytical Psychology*, 32: 93–115.

Plaut, A. (1956) "The Transference in Analytical Psychology", in Fordham, M. *et al.* (eds) *Technique in Jungian Analysis*, London: Heinemann, 1974.

—— (1972) "Analytical Psychologists and Psychological Types: Comment on Replies to a Survey", *Journal of Analytical Psychology*, 17: 137–151.

Quenk, A. and Quenk, N. (1982) "The Use of Psychological Typology in Analysis", in Stein, M. (ed.) *Jungian Analysis*, Boulder: Shambhala.

Racker, H. (1953) "The Countertransference Neurosis", *Transference and Countertransference*, New York: International Universities Press, 1968.

—— (1957) "The Meanings and Uses of Countertransference", *Transference and Countertransference*, New York: International Universities Press, 1968.

—— (1968) *Transference and Countertransference*, New York: International Universities Press.

Samuels, A. (1985) *Jung and the Post-Jungians*, London: Routledge & Kegan Paul.

—— (1989) *The Plural Psyche*, London: Routledge.

—— (1993) *The Political Psyche*, London: Routledge.

Schwartz-Salant, N. (1982) *Narcissism and Character Transformation*, Toronto: Inner City Books.

—— (1984) "Archetypal Factors Underlying Sexual Acting Out in the Transference/Countertransference Process", *Chiron*, 1984: 1–30.

—— (1986) "On the Subtle Body Concept in Clinical Practice", *Chiron*, 1986: 19–58.

—— (1988a) "Before the Creation: The Unconscious Couple in Borderline States of Mind", *Chiron*, 1988: 1–40.

—— (1988b) "Archetypal Foundations of Projective Identification", *Journal of Analytical Psychology*, 33: 39–59.

—— (1989) *The Borderline Personality: Vision and Healing*, Wilmette: Chiron Publications.

—— (1990) "The Abandonment Depression: Developmental and Alchemical Perspectives", *Journal of Analytical Psychology*, 35: 143–159.

Searles, H.F. (1958) "The Schizophrenic's Vulnerability to the Therapist's Unconscious Processes," *Collected Papers on Schizophrenia and Related Subjects*, New York: International Universities Press, 1965.

—— (1959) "Oedipal Love in the Countertransference", *Collected Papers on Schizophrenia and Related Subjects*, New York: International Universities Press, 1965.

—— (1961) "Phases of Patient–Therapist Interaction in the Psychotherapy of Chronic Schizophrenia", *Collected Papers on Schizophrenia and Related Subjects*, New York: International Universities Press, 1965.

—— (1966) "Feelings of Guilt in the Psychoanalyst", *Countertransference and Related Subjects*, New York: International Universities Press, 1979. [Hereafter this book will be referred to as *Countertransference*.]

—— (1967) "The Schizophrenic Individual's Experience of His World", *Countertransference*.

—— (1973) "Some Aspects of Unconscious Fantasy", *Countertransference*.

—— (1975a) "The Patient as Therapist to his Analyst", *Countertransference*.

—— (1975b) "Countertransference and Theoretical Model", *Countertransference*.

—— (1976) "Transitional Phenomena and Therapeutic Symbiosis", *Countertransference*.

—— (1977) "Dual- and Multiple-Identity Processes in Borderline Ego Functioning", *Countertransference*.

—— (1978) "Psychoanalytic Therapy with the Borderline Adult: Some Principles Concerning Technique", in Masterson, J. (ed.) *New Perspectives on the Psychotherapy of the Borderline Adult*, New York: Brunner/Mazel.

—— (1979) *Countertransference and Related Subjects*, New York: International Universities Press.

Sedgwick, D. (1993) *Jung and Searles: A Comparative Study*, London: Routledge.

Singer, J. (1973) *Boundaries of the Soul*, Garden City: Anchor Books.

Smith, M., Glass, G. and Miller, T. (1981) *The Benefits of Psychotherapy*, Baltimore: Johns Hopkins University Press.

Stein, M. (ed.) (1982) *Jungian Analysis*, Boulder: Shambhala.

—— (1984) "Power, Shamanism and Maieutics in the Countertransference", *Chiron*, 1984: 67–87.

Steinberg, W. (1989) "The Therapeutic Utilization of Countertransference", *Quadrant*, 22: 11–26.

Strauss, R. (1960) "Counter-transference", in Fordham, M. *et al.* (eds) *Technique in Jungian Analysis*, London: Heinemann, 1974.

Tansey, M. and Burke, W. (1989) *Understanding Countertransference: From Projective Identification to Empathy*, Hillsdale: The Analytic Press.

Tower, L. (1956) "Countertransference", *Journal of the American Psychoanalytic Association*, 4: 224–255.

Von Franz, M.L. (1974) *Shadow and Evil in Fairytales*, Zurich: Spring Publications.

Weigert, E. (1952) "Contribution to the Problem of Termination in Psychoanalysis", *Psychoanalytic Quarterly*, 21: 465–480.

—— (1954) "Countertransference and Self-Analysis of the Psychoanalyst", *International Journal of Psychoanalysis*, 35: 242–246.

Wheelwright, J. (ed.) (1968) *The Reality of the Psyche*, New York: Putnam's.

—— (ed.) (1971) *The Analytic Process*, New York: Putnam's.

Wickes, F. (1938) *The Inner World of Man*, New York: Farrar and Rinehart. (Re-published 1988, Sigo Press).

Winnicott, D. (1949) "Hate in the Countertransference", *International Journal of Psychoanalysis*, 30: 69–74.

Zinkin, L. (1969) "Flexibility in Analytic Technique", in Fordham, M. *et al.* (eds) *Technique in Jungian Analysis*, London: Heinemann, 1974.

INDEX

acting out 30, 51, 63, 77, 125
active imagination 20, 25, 32, 114
Alder, G. 39
alchemy, used as metaphor 5, 8,
   10, 12–14, 32–33, 34, 36, 105,
   129, 146
analysis: as "dialectical" or
   "reciprocal" process 12, 15, 18,
   27; goals of 106; Jacoby's and
   Schwartz-Salant's definitions
   32; mutuality in 12, 30, 34, 104,
   133; preliminary stages 40–44,
   88–89, 121; process of 145;
   reserve, neutrality in 18, 50, 69,
   100, 142 (see also
   self-disclosure); see also Jungian
   psychology analysis
analyst: centrality of
   psyche/personality of 5, 7, 11,
   12, 16; "clean hands" approach
   10–11, 14, 115, 133 (see also
   training analysis); needs 147;
   reactions to patients 1–2,
   123–124, 136 (see also
   countertransference; empathy);
   safeguards for (Steinberg) 37;
   as selfobject (Kohut) 20, 31;
   sequential listening method
   (Goodheart) 27, 111; stuck 36;
   vulnerability 15, 44, 48, 81, 108,
   112, 134 (see also projection
   "hooks"; wounded healer); see
   also individual therapeutic
   activities

analytic container 44, 45, 99
analytic dialectic (Fordham)18
analytic engagement 89–90,
   122–123
analytic frame 27, 44, 47, 48, 57
analytic marriage 36, 66, 82; see
   also coniunctio
analytic style 137; Jung and 10, 18
anger 96, 98, 138, 141–142;
   patient's see under patient
anima, animus 13, 42, 43, 54, 55,
   62, 132
anthropology, used in Jungian
   analysis 10, 13
anxiety 90, 125, 137, 138
archetypal countertransference
   36, 37
archetypal dreams 23
archetypes 31, 32, 34, 35;
   incarnating (Plaut) 19, 20, 51;
   Jung and 12–13; see also
   wounded healer
Asklepios 15, 24, 25
Attis–Cybele archetype 34

Berlin school 9, 21–24
Bion, W.R. 3, 122
Blomeyer, R. 7, 9, 23, 110
boundaries 43, 44, 49, 52–53, 94,
   95, 112
Brown, J.A.C. 135
Burke, W. 4, 152 n11

Cameron, A. 20

160